'THE MOST EXTRAORDINARY DISTRICT IN THE WORLD'

Ironbridge and Coalbrookdale

By the same author:

Banbury's Poor in 1850 (1966)

A Victorian M.P. and his Constituents (1969)

Drink and Sobriety in an early Victorian country town
(with Dr. B. H. Harrison, 1969)

The Pergamon General Historical Atlas
(with A. C. Cave, 1970)

The Industrial Revolution in Shropshire (1973)

The Darbys of Coalbrookdale (1974)

'The Most Extraordinary District in the World'

IRONBRIDGE and COALBROOKDALE

An anthology of visitors' impressions of
Ironbridge, Coalbrookdale and the Shropshire coalfield

edited with an introduction
by

BARRIE TRINDER

Published in association with
Ironbridge Gorge Museum Trust
by

PHILLIMORE

1977

Published by
PHILLIMORE & CO. LTD.
London and Chichester

Head Office: Shopwyke Hall,
Chichester, Sussex, England

ISBN 0 85033 244 3

Printed in Great Britain by
UNWIN BROTHERS LIMITED
at The Gresham Press, Old Woking, Surrey

CONTENTS

ACKNOWLEDGMENTS

The editor and publisher wish to thank the following for permission to reproduce copyright material, full details of which are given elsewhere:

The Editor and Editorial Board of 'West Midlands Studies', the Polytechnic, Wolverhampton, for extracts II and XXI.

The Librarian, Cambridge University Library, for extract VI.

Miss F. Andrews, for extract VIII.

The Department of Manuscripts, the British Library, for extract X.

C. E. Corbett, Est., and the Salop Record Office, for extract XI.

D. Bradford Barton, Ltd., for extract XIII.

The Pennsylvania State Archives, for extract XV.

The Science Museum, London, for extract XVII.

Mrs. P. Henderson and the Northamptonshire Record Office, for extract XXIV.

The Newcomen Society, for extracts XXV and XXVII.

The Caradoc and Severn Valley Field Club, for extract XXXI.

The Editor of 'The Local Historian' and the Standing Conference for Local History, for extract XXXIII.

LIST OF ILLUSTRATIONS

FOREWORD

THIS ANTHOLOGY OF VISITORS' IMPRESSIONS of Coalbrookdale, Ironbridge and the east Shropshire coalfield in general is intended for three main groups of readers. For local people and the many who live further afield who are interested in the history of a particularly fascinating area it offers an opportunity to gain some acquaintance with one of the main types of evidence on which historians' writings are based. For the multitude of educational groups who visit the district it provides in a convenient and concise form a range of sources which should help in understanding the history of the landscape, and add new meaning to the surviving monuments preserved by the Ironbridge Gorge Museum. For the historian with specialist interests, whether in wage rates, the technology of early railways or revivalism, it gives a selection of material which may stimulate new lines of enquiry or argument, or provide a basis for comparison with other areas.

The main problem in compiling the anthology has been what to omit rather than what to include. I have tried to cater principally for the reader with general rather than particular interests, and so have not, for example, included every visitor's explanation of the workings of the Hay inclined plane or of Lord Dundonald's tar and coke ovens. The source of each extract is clearly indicated, and the reader who wants to follow specialist interests further should be able to do so without too much difficulty.

I am very much aware that the anthology is far from comprehensive and that some important sources are omitted. There must certainly be many 18th-century travel books at present unknown to historians of the district. The journal of the Swede Reinhold Angenstein who visited Coalbrookdale during a tour of England in 1753 is currently being translated and edited, and its publication is eagerly awaited by everyone interested in 18th-century social and economic history. There are other Swedish accounts of east Shropshire, not at present available in English, which are likewise omitted. Further important sources are the journals of the many Quakers who stayed with the ironmasters of Coalbrookdale during the 18th century, but apart from the journal of the paper-maker Joshua Gilpin, I have not included any Quaker diaries in this selection. The pictures in the anthology are but a small proportion of the many which were produced in the late-18th century. In recent years many hitherto unknown paintings and engravings of the district have been located, and it is intended to assemble as many as possible for a major exhibition in 1979 to mark the bicentenary of the Iron Bridge, the catalogue of which should provide a definitive list.

Throughout the anthology the original spelling and punctuation have been retained.

ix

I am grateful, as always, to the many people who have aided my research in various ways, in particular to the publishers and others who have allowed the reproduction of copyright material, and to those who have given help with illustrations. My colleague, Andrew Jenkinson, has kindly provided advice on the geological content of the anthology.

BARRIE TRINDER

INTRODUCTION

IN APRIL 1782 MATTHEW BOULTON of the Soho Manufactory, Birmingham, was writing on steam-engine business to his partner James Watt, who was for the time being away from the town. He explained that a partner from a coal works in Namur was staying with him, and that the following day he would be obliged to take him to Coalbrookdale, which the visitor very much wished to see.[1]

The ambition of the coalowner from Namur was shared by many other tourists, British and foreign, in the late-18th century. The natural beauty of the Severn Gorge was then, as now, spectacular, but it was not just for fine scenery that visitors flocked to Ironbridge and Coalbrookdale. One of the most marked of the great economic changes which began in Great Britain around the middle of the 18th century was the concentration of manufacturing industry on the coalfields, and the Severn Gorge in Shropshire was the first place where it was possible to see a large number of ironworks within a short distance. It was also the scene of many of the most important innovations in the making and use of iron, the invention of the coke-smelting process, the first iron rails, the first iron bridge, the first iron boat, the first steam railway locomotive. Its transport systems, dense networks of railways, tub-boat canals, inclined planes on both railways and waterways, displayed great ingenuity. Visitors were also interested in the attempts made by ironmasters to control the unruly temperaments of their workpeople, by restricting opportunities for drunkenness and Sabbath breaking, enforcing punctuality, and providing churches, chapels and schools. Nowhere in Britain was it possible to see the results of economic and social changes in so spectacular a setting, and any traveller interested in scientific or industrial progress, or in the living conditions of workpeople, would endeavour to include the Coalbrookdale area on his itinerary.

Among the leading British engineers and entrepreneurs who had contacts with the district in the late-18th century were Thomas Telford, William Jessop, Benjamin Outram, Josiah Wedgwood, Richard Trevithick, John Curr, James Watt, Matthew Boulton, and John Loudon McAdam, quite apart from people like the third Abraham Darby, John Wilkinson, Richard and William Reynolds and the ninth Earl Dundonald, who themselves operated works in the Severn Gorge and its vicinity. Many artists were attracted to the district, and those who produced paintings or drawings of scenes in the Gorge included Thomas Rowlandson, Paul Sandby Munn, John Sell Cotman, Philip James de Loutherbourg, Joseph Farington, and J. M. W. Turner.[2]

1

Technological innovations attracted rival entrepreneurs and industrial spies to Shropshire. The area was also visited and written about by many mere seekers after the curious who could claim but a meagre understanding of the structures and processes by which they were amazed. Travel books were numerous in the late-18th century. Robert Southey remarked that if an Englishman spent the summer in any of the mountainous provinces, or ran over to Paris for six weeks, he published the history of his travels.[3] For every tourist who published his reflections on his journeyings, many others kept journals which were not printed in their own lifetimes, but which have subsequently come to light. Coalbrookdale stood near to several of the favoured routes between London and North Wales, which brought to it many of the writers and artists who sought to record their impressions of mountain scenery. The area's innkeepers also claimed that they served the important cross-country route from Bristol and Bath to Lancashire and the ports for Ireland. Thus for the leisured classes for whom travel books were written, a journey to Coalbrookdale did not involve a venture into the dark unknown. It could be no more than a slight detour during a journey undertaken for other purposes.

The vogue for the publication of itineraries was not confined to Great Britain. Descriptions of the Severn Gorge appeared in a variety of languages: Frenchmen, Prussians, Bavarians, Swedes, Venetians, and Americans all left accounts of the district. Some were primarily interested in technology and recorded information available in no other sources. Two Frenchmen, P-C. Lesage and a M. de Givry observed iron railways at Madeley Wood in 1784. A Bavarian, Joseph Ritter von Baader made the only surviving measured drawings of the first types of iron rails.[4] Two Prussian engineers in 1826 made the only reference in print to a dual gauge plateway at Coalbrookdale, of which, in recent years, archaeological evidence has come to light.[5] Jean Dutens, a Frenchman, published in 1819 the most detailed set of drawings of the canal inclined plane at the Hay, and the only surviving drawings of the canal/river interchange at Coalport.[6]

The technological information to be gained from tourists' notebooks and journals is of great importance, since there are few other surviving records of many of the things which they saw. But accounts which contain no such precise information are in other respects equally valuable. It is as satisfying to know how a particular place impressed visitors as a whole, at an important stage in its history, as to learn how a particular machine was constructed. From such descriptions as those by Comasco and Dibdin there emerges an impression of a bustling, energetic riverside community in a spectacular natural setting. These are as much complementary to the detailed technological descriptions as the paintings of Turner or Cotman to the drawings of Jean Dutens.

The Severn Gorge was by no means the only industrial area to attract the attention of tourists in the late-18th century. The Cromford district of Derbyshire, where Richard Arkwright erected the first water-powered cotton-spinning mill in 1771, and followed it by the construction of a new village for his workpeople, was also the subject of much attention in travel books,[7] and, like the Shropshire ironworks, the cotton mills were situated in a spectacular gorge. The iron and coal works of the Wye were also much visited, but more, perhaps by tourists passing by boat from Ross to Monmouth for the sake of the scenery than by those who first concern was technology.[8] The Duke of Bridgewater's Canal in Lancashire was also regarded as a curiosity to be visited, and many of those who saw it travelled along it on the Duke's packet boats.[9] The cotton-spinning settlement at New Lanark, in a deep gorge and near to the Falls of Clyde, was an attraction to visitors even before Robert Owen's communitarian experiments made it a place of major concern to everyone with an interest in social change.[10]

By the beginning of the 17th century[11] the Severnside parishes of Benthall, Broseley, and Madeley were renowned for their coalmines, and the ease of transportation by river made the district one of the most prosperous coalfields in Great Britain. Its technological pre-eminence is shown by its early adoption of the wooden railway, in 1605, or a little earlier, and by the development of the longwall method of mining in the district about the middle of the century. By 1700 the manufacture of pottery, bricks, tobacco pipes, glass, salt, and tar was established in the coalfield. The area had long connections with iron-making, for several of the local monasteries had bloomery smithies at the time of the Dissolution, and in the early 17th century Sir Basil Brooke pioneered important innovations in steel-making at Coalbrookdale,[12] but while mineral fuel could not be used in most iron-making processes, the main importance of the coalfield in the iron trade was as a source of iron ore, which was smelted at Coalbrookdale, Kemberton, Leighton Wombridge, Willey, and other water-powered blast furnaces on its periphery.

This situation changed profoundly in the 18th century. In 1708 the first Abraham Darby leased the then derelict blast furnace at Coalbrookdale, and the following year for the first time succeeded in smelting iron ore using coke as his fuel instead of the traditional charcoal. For various reaons this innovation was not quickly adopted in other ironworks, and it made little immediate difference to the area as a whole. The Coalbrookdale ironworks steadily increased in importance, however, manufacturing such products as steam engine cylinders, domestic hollow-ware, railway wheels and architectural ironwork. It was the first ironworks to employ a steam engine to re-circulate water in its pools system. By the early 1750s the works was already attracting visitors. Some, like Charles Wood (Extract II) or the Swede Reinhold Angenstein, who made a visit there in 1753,[13] were interested in ironmaking technology, but others, like Richard Pococke, Bishop of Meath (Extract I) were attracted by the scenic properties of the district, by the curious combination of a rugged natural landscape and awe-inspiring man-made machines and processes, which was so much in accord with the aesthetic tastes of the late-18th century. It was the beauties of the landscape and not metallurgical innovations which led George Perry to publish the first engravings of Coalbrookdale in 1758.

In the late 1750s the pace of economic change in the Shropshire coalfield increased.[14] In 1755 the second Abraham Darby and his partner Thomas Goldney blew in a new blast furnace at Horsehay in the parish of Dawley, about two miles from Coalbrookdale. This was the first coke-using furnace which was fully competitive with furnaces in which charcoal was used. Its output was as great as that of the largest charcoal-using furnaces, and it produced pig iron which could be forged into a good quality wrought iron. At Coalbrookdale, in the decades after iron was first smelted with coke in 1709, the output of the furnaces had been much lower than that of most charcoal-using furnaces, and the pig iron produced had been suitable only for making castings. The success of the Horsehay works was soon imitated. Four other major ironworks were established in east Shropshire by 1759.

The growth of the iron trade slackened in the 1760s, but in the last quarter of the 18th century new blast furnaces and forges came into operation in the district every few years, and by 1802 Thomas Telford could remark with justification that the number of blast furnaces between Ketley and Willey exceeded any within the same space in the kingdom (Extract XX). This was the period of the Iron Bridge, of the introduction of iron rails on railways and inclined planes on canals, of experiments with chemical processes like Dundonald's tar and coke ovens and alkali manufacture at Wombridge, and of the introduction of new industries, like glass-making at Wrockwardine Wood, and porcelain manufacture at Caughley and Coalport. It was a period when many of the local entrepreneurs were men of national standing, and when they had contacts with leading figures in all walks of life. Richard Reynolds, the saintly and restrained Quaker patriarch, lived at Coalbrookdale and Ketley from his first settlement in Shropshire in 1756 until 1804. He was a philanthropist of national reputation, the anonymous distributor of large sums to the poor of Bristol and London, and an active member of the anti-Slavery movement. His son, William, the grandson of the second Abraham Darby, was perhaps the most intellectually able of all of the Shropshire ironmasters. In his early 20s he negotiated with Matthew Boulton and James Watt over the installation of steam engines in the Coalbrookdale partners' ironworks. He was, more than any other individual, responsible for the building of the effective and economical tub boat canal system which served the coalfield. He was the founder of the 'new town' at the terminus of the Shropshire Canal at Coalport, and planned with Lord Dundonald to build there a huge integrated chemical works. He was an enthusiastic geologist, collected information on a wide range of technologies, and experimented with the use of hydrocarbons to drive engines. Reynolds was well acquainted with Archdeacon Joseph Plymley, and through Plymley[15] met such people as Archibald Alison, the Scots philosopher and theologian, and Thomas Clarkson, the anti-Slavery agitator. It was William Reynolds, together with T. C. Eyton, who introduced to Plymley the young Dr. Dugard, who contributed to Plymley's book an account of the Wombridge chemical works. Plymley also entertained at his house the young Thomas Telford, who was well acquainted with both Reynolds and Eyton through his canal interests. The Archdeacon met Arthur Young and William Wilberforce when in London, visited Josiah Wedgwood at Etruria, and stayed with the Rathbone family at Greenbank near Liverpool. The Rathbones, in turn, were related to the Darby and Reynolds families of Coalbrookdale. William Rathbone had married William Reynolds's sister, and Joseph Rathbone his cousin, Mary Darby. In many enterprises, canal promotions, turnpike trusts, the Iron Bridge partnership, the Darbys and Reynoldses came into contact with John Wilkinson, who had extensive iron-making interests in Shropshire, as well as in North Wales and South Staffordshire. Richard Reynolds once referred to Wilkinson in a letter to Boulton and Watt as 'my friend', and was once represented by him at a meeting of the proprietors of the *Tontine* hotel. Wilkinson was perhaps the outstanding ironmaster of the time, a national figure of great importance, but also an active participant in the public life of the Shropshire coalfield.

In the last quarter of the 18th century it was not so much the ironworks but one of their most spectacular products, the first iron bridge, which attracted visitors to the Severn Gorge. The bridge was erected under the supervision of the third Abraham Darby in the summer of 1779, and opened on New Year's Day 1781. In the 20th century it is difficult to appreciate the astonishment and wonder with which the bridge was regarded at the time it was built. No visitor failed to mention it, it formed the centrepiece of numerous paintings and engravings of the Gorge, and it adorned porcelain tankards, the ash-holes of kitchen grates, the Coalbrookdale Company's trade tokens, and the seal of the Shropshire Canal Company. Its fame was not eclipsed by the erection of a much larger bridge at Sunderland in 1795–96, for visitors still felt that they should see both and compare them.

By the late 1790s few visitors to the Ironbridge Gorge failed to see the variety of curiosities in the new settlement at its eastern end which had gained the name of Coalport. Until the last quarter of the century most of the wharves in the Gorge were at its eastern or Coalbrookdale end, but the building of a bridge between the Sheepwash (now Coalport) and Preens Eddy, opened in 1780, stimulated shipping activities in the area. The bridge proprietors were empowered to build wharves and warehouses adjacent to the bridge, and they constructed approach roads from Broseley and Brockton. In 1786 William Reynolds began to drive a level into the side of the Gorge about half a mile upstream from the bridge, and discovered a spring of natural bitumen which was commercially exploited, the level receiving the name of the Tar Tunnel. The original purpose of the level was to serve as an underground canal to bring out the produce of mines on Blists Hill, but on the discovery of the bitumen this intention was abandoned, although it was used for bringing out coal after a railway was laid through it in 1796.[16] In the early 1790s the Shropshire Canal was built, a tub boat waterway, extending seven miles from Donnington Wood in the north of the coalfield, to descend the side of the Severn Gorge by an inclined plane near the Hay Farm. This was one of six inclined planes on the local canal system, and was neither quite the longest nor the steepest. It was the most spectacular, and it was the one most visited, although some tourists recorded their impressions of the Windmill Farm or Stirchley incline further north, which they encountered on their way from Coalbrookdale to Shifnal. The Shropshire Canal below the Hay incline ran parallel with the river for about half a mile to terminate near the bridge at the Sheepwash. The canal/river interchange soon gained the name of Coalport. In this area William Reynolds developed what amounted to a new town,[17] taking responsibility for roads, housing and the ferry service to Jackfield, and encouraging the growth of new industries like chain-making, boat-building, and above all porcelain manufacture. The Preens Eddy bridge underwent many changes. Originally a wooden structure, it was rebuilt on three sets of cast-iron ribs following damage caused by the flood of 1795, and in 1818 was reconstructed wholly in iron. Coalport remained for many years an unusually busy and interesting place, and as late as 1832 the aged Thomas Telford travelling from Woverhampton to Shrewsbury made a detour in order to show its sights to a fellow engineer.[18]

The typical traveller visiting the Severn Gorge in the late-18th century would stay at the *Tontine,* the inn at the north end of the Iron Bridge erected by a consortium which included most of the bridge proprietors. He would closely examine the bridge itself, and might cross it to look at the big waterwheel at Benthall. He might go to the Coalbrookdale ironworks to watch the making of a casting or the tapping of a blast furnace. If he took a serious interest in iron-making, he might also visit the Coalbrookdale forges, the Madeley Wood furnaces alongside the Severn, or the Ketley ironworks further north, where William Reynolds's many innovations were usually shielded from the attention of unknown tourists. If a visitor were scientifically minded he might be invited to visit William Reynolds's laboratory at Ketley Bank House, or to examine the ironmaster's collection of fossils. Many visitors went to see cannon being bored at Alexander Brodie's Calcutts ironworks, by the banks of the Severn in Broseley parish, and to look at Lord Dundonald's coke and tar ovens which lay behind Brodie's furnaces. From Calcutts it was a short journey over the river by ferry to Coalport, where penetrating the Tar Tunnel could be relied upon to stimulate those with a classical education to produce appropriate similes. Both engineers and those who merely enjoyed the spectacular could gain enjoyment from watching or even riding upon the Hay inclined plane. From the mid-1790s the prospect of buying porcelain, or watching it being made, provided a further attraction at Coalport. A further source of amazement to visitors was Lincoln Hill, the cliff of silurian limestone which stands between Coalbrookdale and the town of Ironbridge. On the west side of the hill Richard Reynolds had laid out 'Sabbath Walks', decorated with shrubs and rustic seats, with the intention of diverting his workpeople from public houses on Sundays. At the extremity of the hill the walks culminated in the Rotunda, a bandstand-like construction in cast-iron, which gave extensive views of the Severn Valley, and from which it was possible to observe operations in a vast cavern filled with limekilns, from which extended adits penetrating the pillar-and-stall mine workings in the limestone. The Rotunda was pulled down in February 1804,[19] probably because it was in danger of collapse from subsidence, and the whole shape of the hill has since been considerably altered, both by falls and by tipping.[20] Fortunately not all of the visitors to the coalfield confined their attention to the Iron Bridge and the spectacular attractions around it, and the Wrockwardine Wood inclined plane, the Snedshill ironworks, the remarkable exposure of basalt near Doseley and the Wombridge chemical works were among the sites of interest discovered by those who ventured further afield.

Evangelical religion brought as many visitors to the Ironbridge Gorge in the late-18th century as spectacular scenery or engineering innovations. The presence of John Fletcher as vicar of Madeley from 1760 to 1785, and of his wife who survived him and lived at the vicarage until 1815, brought to the district many of the leading figures in the Evangelical Revival. Fletcher was born Jean Guillaume de la Flechère at Nyon on Lake Geneva in 1729, and migrated to England in 1752 to take up an appointment as tutor to the Hill family at Attingham Park, Shropshire. It was through the Hills that, after ordination in the Church of England, he became vicar of Madeley in 1760. Fletcher was a theologian and controversialist of major importance. He was a close associate of John Wesley, who regarded him, in spite of his poor health, as his own designated successor. Wesley visited Madeley several times during Fletcher's ministry, and paid several further visits after his death. Fletcher, like Wesley, was a Methodist and at the same time an ordained priest of the Church of England, and the close links between Madeley parish church and the local Wesleyan Methodists were maintained until the 1830s. Religious activities in the parish were organised in the period after Fletcher's death in 1785 by Mary Fletcher, the curate of the parish church, and the Wesleyan ministers in the Shrewsbury circuit. The description of a typical Sunday in Madeley by William Tranter gives a vivid impression of the period. Throughout the 19th century Methodists and other Evangelicals visited Madeley to gain inspiration from the scenes of Fletcher's ministry, and numerous engravings of the vicarage, the church, and Fletcher's bedroom were produced for sale.

It is not surprising in an area whose prosperity depended on its mineral wealth that visitors should have taken a more than usual interest in the local geology. The earliest travellers would not have realised the real significance of their observations, but most were factually accurate so far as they went. The hand-working methods of both mining and quarrying were more conducive to the finding of good fossil specimens than the mechanical means used today, and the collection of fossils or 'figured stones' was a popular 18th-century pastime. References are made to the proximity of all the necessary raw materials, coal, ironstone and limestone, which rendered Coalbrookdale so suitable a location for the development of the iron industry, but, especially in the early accounts, there is naturally no appreciation of just how fortuitous this coincidence is. The limestone of Lincoln Hill and Benthall Edge is of Silurian age, some 100 million years older than the Coal Measures. The 'large reeds' referred to by Pococke would almost certainly be the ribbed and flattened stems of *Calamites,* a tree-like ancestor of our modern horsetails, while 'the bark of trees' would be the stems of the large ferns of *Lepidodenron* and *Sigillaria* type. *'Conchae amoniae',* although described as a vivalve, probably refers to the coiled gastropod shell, *Poleumita* from the limestone, a fairly common fossil which even today is often confused with the much later true ammonites. *'Eruca anthropomorphe'* described at Dudley, is difficult to trace. It has no modern meaning and might be either animal or plant, but if the implication is that it came from the limestone at Dudley, it could be a coral of some kind. The fossil in Miss Ford's collection with 'legs spread out like a millipede' is almost certainly a plant; one of the ferns with rather spikey leaves or branches.

George Perry clearly differentiates, without specific reference to age, between the shells and corals of the limestone and the plants which are found mainly in ironstone nodules. The hand-sorting of the latter by women and children would lead to many discoveries of these fossils, which are usually very well preserved. That Joshua Gilpin should notice the columnar basalt is most interesting, since, while it is conspicuous today in Doseley quarry where it has been exploited for road metal, it is uncertain where he could have obtained a good view of it in 1796. Possibly one of the roads in the Doseley area had worn down to the top surface of the basalt which would have revealed its noticeably polygonal structure. Gilpin's reference to alternating strata of limestone and sandstone is rather obscure. The most geologically accurate account is that by Robert Townson, who, among his many other interests, made something of a speciality of the study of mineralogy.

After 1810 the Shropshire iron industry suffered a relative decline. As other areas like South Wales and the Black Country increased their production, the rate of growth in Shropshire slackened. In the depression which followed the peace of 1815, the Shropshire works, with much of their equipment by then obsolete, suffered more severely than those elsewhere. The accounts of Thomas Butler and Joshua Field give a vivid picture of the dereliction of those years. After 1822 there was a revival of the iron trade, but the new works of the 19th century were to the north and east of the coalfield, at the Lodge, Priorslee, Stirchley, Hinkshay, Langley Field, Madeley Court and Blists Hill. With the exception of the latter, blast furnaces disappeared from the Ironbridge Gorge and its immediate vicinity, although the Coalbrookdale ironworks continued as a foundry, and was reckoned by 1851 to be the largest in Great Britain. It specialised in the production of high-quality castings, and gained a particular high reputation for its cast-iron art work. The 1850s saw the beginnings of a large-scale decorative tile industry in the Gorge, which to some extent compensated for the decline of ironmaking. In spite of these developments, foreign visitors to Britain in the mid-19th century were no longer interested in industrial Shropshire. Manchester, and later Birmingham, became the chief objects of their attention.[21] Such writers as de Tocqueville, Taine, Faucher, and Engels fail to mention the Ironbridge Gorge, which they most certainly would have visited had they come to England in 1800. Most accounts of industrial Shropshire in the 19th century come therefore from local sources.

The whole of the Shropshire coalfield began to decline in the 1870s, and revival on a significant scale has only begun with the designation of the new town of Telford in the area in the 1960s. The final extracts in this selection are therefore a report of a speech in 1871, which is rather like the Swan Song of the Shropshire iron industry, and an article which prophesied the preservation for posterity of the monuments of the late-18th century, a prediction which has happily come to fulfilment in the 1970s.

REFERENCES

1. Matthew Boulton–James Watt, 13 April 1782, Birmingham Reference Library, Boulton and Watt Collection, parcel 'D'.
2. Barrie Trinder, *The Industrial Revolution in Shropshire* (1973), pp. 181–182, 188–191.
3. Robert Southey, *Letters from England*, ed. by J. Simmons (1951), p. 15.
4. P. J. Wexler, *La Formation du vocabulaire des Chemins de Fer en France* (1788-1842) (1955), p. 19; Joseph von Baader, *Neues System de Fortschaffendem Mechanik* (1822).
5. See Extract XXVII.
6. Jean Dutens, *Memoirs sur les Travaux Publiques d'Angleterre* (1819).
7. *The Torrington Diaries*, ed. by C. B. Andrews (1954), pp. 178–182, 251–253; (Anon.) Thomas Newte, *A Tour of England and Scotland by an English Gentleman* (1788), pp. 25–30; Rev. Richard Warner, *A Tour through the Northern Counties* (1802), Vol. I, pp. 143–144; *The Farington Diary*, ed. by James Greig (1922), Vol. I, p. 314.
8. W. Mavor, *A Tour in Wales and through Several Counties of England performed in the summer of 1805* (1806), pp. 22–27; Samuel Ireland, *Picturesque Views of the River Wye* (1797), *passim*; L. Simond, *Journal of a Tour and Residence in Great Britain during the years 1810 and 1811 by a French Traveller* (1815), Vol. I, p. 207; *The Farington Diary, op cit.*, Vol. II, pp. 149-150; E. I. Spence, *Summer Excursions through parts of Oxfordshire, Gloucestershire, etc.* (1809), Vol. I, p. 63.
9. Thomas Newte, *op. cit.*, pp. 42–44; H. M. Rathbone, ed., *The Letters of Richard Reynolds* (1852), pp. 93–94; R. Warner, *op cit.*, Vol. II, pp. 153–56.

10. L. Simond, *op. cit.*, Vol. I, p. 278.
11. For a summary of economic developments in the area in the 17th century *see* Barrie Trinder, *op. cit.*, pp. 5–32.
12. Malcolm Wanklyn, 'Iron and Steelworks in Coalbrookdale in 1645' in *Shropshire Newsletter*, No. 44, 1973.
13. M. W. Flinn, 'The Travel Diaries of Swedish Engineers of the 18th century as sources of Technological History', in *Transactions of the Newcomen Society*, XXXI (1957–59), p. 104.
14. This period is summarised in Barrie Trinder, *op. cit.*, pp. 33–47, 54–80.
15 Diaries of Katherine Plymley, Shropshire Record Office p. 567.
16. I. J. Brown and Barrie Trinder, *The Coalport Tar Tunnel* (1971).
17. Barrie Trinder, *op. cit.*, pp. 216–224.
18. Sir Alexander Gibb, *The Story of Telford* (1935), p. 281.
19. The Diary of Thomas Boycott, Shopshire Record Office, 245/14.
20. I. J. Brown, *A History of Limestone Mining in Shropshire* (1967), pp. 17–20.
21. Asa Briggs, *Victorian Cities* (1968), pp. 88-138, 184-240.

I

Richard Pococke (1704–65) was Bishop of the Irish dioceses of Ossory and Meath. He travelled in Egypt, Palestine, Greece, and the Alps, and published accounts of his journeys, although it was not until the late 19th century that his detailed diaries of his travels in Great Britain between 1747 and 1760 appeared in print. His account of 1751 describes the Severn Gorge before the main onset of industrialisation, and shows that one of the daughters of Richard Ford, manager of the Coalbrookdale ironworks, had an interest in geology. In the 1757 account, 'Penslarn' would appear to be corruption of Priorslee, while the source in 'Dauly' (Dawley) from which iron for the Lydeat forges was obtained would have been the Horsehay furnaces.

Source: *The Travels through England of the Rev. Richard Pococke, II.* Camden Society 1888/9, ed. J. J. Cartwright, Vol. I, pp. 230–232, Vol. II, p. 290.

17 June 1851.

(From Stourbridge) . . . Descending from this country we soon came into Shropshire a little beyond the New Inn, having had a view of Gataker towards the Severn. We passed over the river Worfe, which falls into the Severn near Bridgnorth, and coming into the woody country, I went through a small village called Madely or Madely Wood. This parish extends to the Severn, and on the banks of that river is a considerable village which extends up the steep cliffs over the river. I was here recommended to a gentleman who conducted me along the height over the river by the quarries of lime-stone, and particularly by that hill which is called Lincoln Hill, and is most remarkable for figured fossils, which they find in all these parts, particularly the bivalve Conchae amoniae and others, coralline substances, large reeds, and barks of trees, cones of firr trees and plants inclosed mostly in iron-stones and others, and the Eruca anthropomorphe described at Dudley. I here saw Miss Ford's collection, and in it one or two faces of a stone which was broken in two in which there is a plain appearance of legs, spreading out, much like those of the millipedes. I saw one very different from the others and small, the head much like the head of a hawk, and covered with little nodules or knobs as some of the spiculae of the echinus are, which have been found in the chalk pits. At the ironworks here I saw octagon ovens of cast iron from three to four feet long, and about 18 in. diameter, to be

1. '... the ground being high and steep, varied with wood houses, and the coal machinery, for the other side much abounds in coal. ...' (Richard Pococke, 1751)

A View of the mouth of a Coal Pit near Broseley in Shropshire (Francis Chesham, 1788)

Ironbridge Gorge Museum Trust

2. '... We came ... to where the collieries begin ... to Watling Street collieries, being on each side of the road. ...' (Richard Pococke, 1751)

Watling Street and the northern part of the Shropshire coalfield, from John Rocque's Map of Shropshire, 1752

put at the back of kitchen chimneys. Nothing can be imagined more roman-
tick and beautiful than the views of the Severn when one is on these heights,
which far exceeds the prospects on the river; the ground being high and
steep, varied with wood houses, and the coal machinery, for the other side
much abounds in coal. A rivlet runs down by the ironworks at Madeley
Wood, not represented in the map, and from the place where it falls into
the Severn, I went along by the banks of the Severn up the river two miles
to Bildwas Bridge . . .

June 1757 . . .

We went from Tong and passed by Lydeat forges for making bars of iron,
the ore being found and smelted at Dauly, and in about two miles came into
the high road from London to Shrewsbury. We saw to the right Weston
Hall, Lord Bradford's, and in 7 miles from Tong came to Penslarn where
the collieries begin. It is a large coal, burns swift and is very cheap, and from
this colliery they are supplyed very much down the Severn. We soon came
to Watling Street collieries, being on each side of the road. This place has its
name from the old Watling Street which is the Roman way from Dover to
Cardigan . . . this name continues to Wellington where our Turnpike goes
to Shrewsbury; and the other towards Wem in which road we went and
immediately came to the end of the poor town of Wellington, on the foot
of the Wrekin which on this side appears a very beautiful hill.

II

Charles Wood was an ironmaster, who, along with a fellow ironmaster, Gabriel Griffiths, undertook a tour of the West Midlands in 1754, during which he kept a diary detailing the processes he saw in use at ironworks they visited. At Coalbrookdale he met the then clerk, Richard Ford II, from whom he received a gloomy account of the prospects for the area which was to be confounded in following decades. The account of the Coalbrookdale ironworks is of particular value for the information it reveals about the early use of coke in forging processes, and its revelation that stamper heads and shanks for Cornish tin mines were made there. The claim that coke blast iron had been used for making wrought iron for 30 years is not borne out by the works accounts. This is the only source to reveal the existence of a steam engine at the ironworks at Leighton (Layton). The name of the owner of the first forge in Coalbrookdale was Thomas Hallen, not Thomas Allen.

Source: Charles K. Hyde, 'The Iron Industry of the West Midlands in 1754; Observations from the Travel Account of Charles Wood', The Polytechnic, Wolverhampton, *Journal of West Midlands Studies,* VI (1973), pp. 39–40.

Monday, September 16th.

Called at the Dale. The first Forge belongs to Mr. Thomas Allen, which is employed in plating for Frying pans, fire shovels, etc. All their damaged plates are made into Chafing dishes, as the small pieces will serve for some part of them.

The next Water work is a Mill for Boring their large fire Engine Cylindors. The next above, is a forge, with 2 finerys and a Chafery. The finerys are employ'd in Sinking pit coal pigs, & they say they make 1½ ton Weekly Single hand. The next Work above i.e. Coalbrookdale is a furnace for castings, they say they make 12 tons Weekly and can make the Pigs of any grain they please. They have made Mill Iron from Coke pigs, with Charcoal for 30 years. And the Scarcity and great demand for those Pigs induced them to erect more furnaces as they bear a good price. The vein of Coal that they make use of for Coking is not than two feet thick. Their Ironstone measure is thick. But Mr. Ford things that both Coal & Ironstone will fail in 20 years, so that it will not be worth anyones while to continue, or Erect other works there. He informs me that (they) have made Stamper heads &

Shanks for the Stamper houses in Cornwall, of wrought iron made in a finery with the small Coke that they could not use in their furnaces, from their Coke metal & he let me see some of them, which appeared clean & good. Above this Furnace there is another, which makes the same quantity of Castings with Coke. Mr. Ford says that they Employ about 250 hands, besides Carriers, etc. The castings are taken by the Workmen at a certain price per ton. Their Bellows are 20 feet long. Blow hard, & have a good Blast. The Coal they use to Coke is call'd Clod Coal, & is a weak coal for the strong & hot will not do. The Coke made of it is near as light as Wood Coal. Their Stack is nearly the same Dimensions as other furnaces, as Mr. Ford informs me.

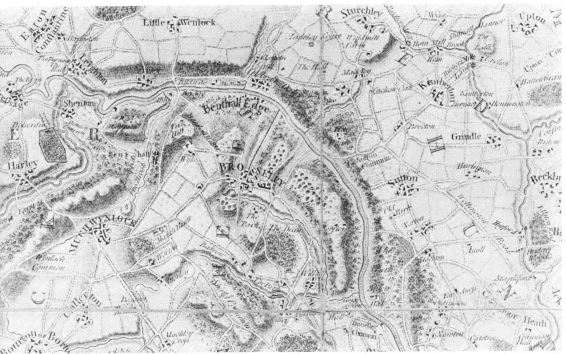

'... The first Forge belongs to Mr. Thomas Allan. ... The next Water work is a Mill for Boring. ... The xt Work above i.e. Coalbrookdale is a furnace for castings. ... Layton Furnace lyes about 2 miles from Buildwas Bridge. ...' (Charles Wood, 1754)

The Severn Gorge, from John Rocque's Map of Shropshire, 1752

Salop County Record Office

Layton Furnace lyes about 2 miles from Buildways Bridge. Blows with Charcoal, belongs to Mr. Ford. They make 20 Ton weekly through the Blast, this he says is from an improvement he has made in the Structure of it. The water is raised by a fire Engine & runs into the Pool again, in the same manner they do at the Dale, otherways (*sic*) they would not have water sufficient. There is the most work done at these places, with the least water, of any place in England.

15

III

The earliest known published views of Coalbrookdale are two engravings by Francis Vivares of drawings by Thomas Smith of Derby and George Perry which appeared in 1758 (see Plates 4 and 5). A prospectus for the engravings was written by George Perry (1719–71), who lived in Coalbrookdale, and was the principal partner in the Lightmoor ironworks, set up in 1758. While Perry's account says nothing of the vast changes in the Shropshire iron trade which were taking place at the time it was written, it bears impressive witness to the steady progress which has been made at Coalbrookdale itself over the previous 40 years. The original prospectus was reputedly one of the first jobs undertaken by the great printer and typographer, John Baskerville.

Source: G. Perry, 'A Description of Coalbrookdale . . . with perspective views thereof', n.d., *c.* 1758.

A DESCRIPTION of COALBROOKDALE in the County of SALOP, with two Perspective VIEWS thereof.

The PROPRIETORS are under Engagement to give their SUBSCRIBERS a Description of COALBROOKDALE, a task which they find it no easy matter to execute as they could wish. Amidst a great variety of things which well deserve the attention of those who are curious in the works of Nature, or of Art, it is difficult to select such for particular notice, as may best suit with all Tastes, and to attempt a minute detail of each, might perhaps seem tedious, and would certainly run this description to a much greater length than is consistent with the Authors' design. They shall think themselves happy therefore, if by a short and general Account, they can give their Readers any tolerable idea of a place so remarkable, that it is presum'd few Persons of Curiosity who have taken the pains to examin it on the spot, have ever found themselves disappointed.

The VILLAGE derives its Name from its situation in a low Valley surrounded on every side by high Hills, thro' the Midst of which runs a small Rivulet, which from its rise among the Coal-mines, is call'd COALBROOK, and which after it has been employ'd through the whole Valley in driving a number of Water-Wheels, loses itself about half a mile below, in the River Severn. COALBROOKDALE is situated in the Parish of Madeley, and Franchise of Wenlock, from which it is distant about Six Statute Miles, five from Wellington and Shifnal, nine from Bridgnorth, and Fourteen from

4. '. . . *there are perhaps few places where rural Prospects, and scenes of hurry and Business are so happily united as at Coalbrookdale. . . .*' (George Perry, *c.* 1758)

The South West Prospect of Coalbrookdale and the adjacent Country (Thomas Smith & T. Vivares, *c.* 1758)

Ironbridge Gorge Museum Trust

Shrewsbury, the Reakin (a Celebrated Hill in Shropshire) lying to the North West at about Three Miles distance.

ALL the adjacent Country abounds with mines. Those of Coal are the most numerous, but the same which produce coal afford likewise great Quantities of Ironstone, and (as if Nature had intended this place for an Iron Foundery) Limestone the proper Flux for Iron, is found in great Plenty in the Neighbourhood, Lincoln Hill, just to the South of the Dale, is a huge Rock of Limestone, in a long tract of Time this Hill has been cut hollow to a great Depth, so that the top of it now appears like a vast Pit, Four hundred and forty yards long and fifty two wide, each side being a frightful Precipice.

BESIDES the natural Production of these Mines, other extraneous Bodies found in them, have been throught worth the notice of those who are fond of Natural History. Abundance of Fossil Shells and Corals etc. of divers kinds, are daily dug up in the Limestone Quarries, and in some Nodules of Ironstone are found perfect Impressions of the leaves of Fern and other Plants, and sometimes (tho' more rarely) Cones of Fire and other vegetable Productions are found bedded in the stone. These have been of late Years much in Request, and have found a place in the Cabinets of the most curious Persons.

17

IN a Situation so well furnish'd with all the necessary Materials, one might naturally enough expect a Manufactory of Iron, and yet it is but of late years that this Branch of Business has been brought to its present flourishing state there. In the year One Thousand Seven Hundred, the whole Village consisted of only One Furnace, Five Dwelling Houses, and a Forge or two, about Forty Years ago the present Iron-foundry was establish'd, and since that time its Trade and Buildings are so far increas'd that it contains at least Four Hundred and Fifty inhabitants, and finds employment for more than Five hundred People, including all the several Occupations that are connected with the Works.

THE Face of the Country shews the happy Effects of this flourishing Trade, the lower class of People who are very numerous here, are enabled to live comfortably; their Cottages, which almost cover some of the neighbouring Hills, are throng'd with healthy Children, who soon are able to find Employment, and perhaps chearfulness and contentment are not more visible in any other place. A pleasing Proof this, that Arts and Manufactures contribute greatly to the Wealth and power of a Nation, and that Industry and Commerce will soon improve and People the most uncultivated Situation.

THIS place affords a number of delightful prospects. One might venture to say that all the Principal Beauties of landscape may be observ'd from some or other of the Hills that surround it. Some of the Hills are cover'd with Verdure, others overgrown with Wood, and some again are naked and barren. These, with a View of a fine fertile Country, Water'd by the Severn, all contribute to form as agreeable a Variety to the Eye, as can well be conceiv'd. The Beauty of the scene is in the mean time greatly increas'd by a near view of the Dale itself, Pillars of Flame and smoke rising to vast

5. *'. . . Pillars of Flame and smoke rising to vast height, large Reservoirs of Water, and a number of Engines in motion. . . .'* (George Perry, c. 1758)
A View of the Upper Works at Coalbrookdale (George Perry & T. Vivares, c. 1758)

height, large Reservoirs of Water, and a number of Engines in motion, never fail to raise the admiration of strangers, tho' it must be confess'd these things join'd to the murmuring of the Waterfalls, the noise of the Machines, and the roaring of the Furnaces, are apt to occasion a kind of Horror in those who happen to arrive in a dark Night. UPON the whole, there are perhaps few Places where rural Prospects, and Scenes of hurry and Business are so happily united as at COALBROOKDALE. Barren Rocks, Hills and Woodlands, put one in mind at first sight, of the lonely Retreats of Melancholy and Contemplation, whilst the work in the Valley, the hurry and Crowd of the Inhabitants, and the various Employments of the Workmen, display a lively view of one of the most active Scenes of Business that can be imagined.

PLATE I Exhibits a near prospect of the upper works, the top of the Perspective house, on the summit of the Hill is about Two Hundred Feet above the surface of the Pool. From this Station several principal Houses are seen, belonging to the Proprietors, also several Furnaces, and near the foreground is represented a large Cylinder on its Carriage, supposed to be Seventy Inches Diameter, Ten Feet Long and weighing about Six Tons being the Real Dimensions of one lately cast at this Foundery and sent to Cornwall.

PLATE II is taken from the Top of a Precipice called the White-Rock, including a general View of the Dale, and Adjacent Country, looking South West, Mr. Darby's house appears in the front, and the Works deep sunk in the Valley to the left hand, beyond which, Lincoln Hill, with several breaches cut thro' it, appears like an old Encampment; over it is seen a part of Broseley Town, and the Prospect is terminated by a distant View of the Brown Clee, and Church Stretton Hills.

HOW far the Proprietors may have succeeded in their attempts to Represent active and still life united in one Scene, must be submitted to the Publick. In the mean Time they beg leave to return thanks to all such Persons of Quality, and Gentry, who by the following Subscription have encouraged the Publication of a Work originally intended only for private Amusement.

19

IV

George Perry was also the author of an account of barge traffic on the river Severn, published in 1758. Records of the barge traffic are very sparse, and Perry's account forms the basis of much of what has subsequently been written about it. Perhaps the most valuable feature of his description is his census of barges and owners taken in 1756, which shows very clearly the great concentration of barge-owners in Bridgnorth and the ports of the Gorge.

Source: *Gentlemen's Magazine,* Vol. 28, 1758, p. 277.

This river, being justly esteemed the second in Britain, is of great importance on account of its trade, being navigated by vessels of large burden more than 160 miles from the sea, without the assistance of any lock; upwards of 100,000 tons of coals are annually shipped from the collieries about Broseley and Madeley to the towns situated on its banks, and from thence into the adjacent countries: also great quantities of grain, pig and bar iron, iron manufactures and earthenwares; as well as wool, hops, cyder and provisions, are constantly exported to Bristol and other places, from whence merchants' goods are brought in return. The freight from Shrewsbury to Bristol is about 10s. per ton, and from Bristol to Shrewsbury 15s., the rates to the intermediate towns being in proportion.

This traffic is carried with vessels of two sorts:—

the lesser kind are called barges and frigates, being from 40 to 60 feet in length, have a single mast, square sail and carry from 20 to 40 tons;

the trows or larger vessels are from 40 to 80 tons burthen; these have a main and top mast, about 80 feet high, with square sails, and some have mizzen masts; they are generally from 16 to 20 feet wide, and 60 feet in length, being, when new and completely rigged, worth about £300.

Their number being greatly increased of late, I commissioned in May 1756, an exact list to be taken of all the barges and trows upon the River Severn, whereby the increase or diminution of its trade may be estimated in future times, which are as follows:—

20

Belonging to	Owners	Vessels
Welshpool & Pool Stake	4	4
Shrewsbury	10	19
Cound & Buildwas	3	7
Madeley Wood	21	39
Benthall	8	13
Broseley	55	87
Bridgnorth	47	75
Between it & Bewdley	8	10
Bewdley	18	47
Between it & Worcester	7	13
Worcester	6	21
Between it & Upton	2	2
Upton	5	5
Tewkesbury	8	18
Evesham (Avon)	1	2
The Hawe	3	4
Gloucester	4	7
Totals	210	376

V

John Fletcher, vicar of Madeley, was one of the leading figures in the religious life of 18th-century England, an eminent theologian, controversialist and pamphleteer, and at the same time a priest who showed an extraordinary degree of concern for the morals of his parishioners. Fletcher was born at Nyon on Lake Geneva, and came to England in 1752 as tutor to the family of Thomas Hill of Tern Hall, Atcham. Subsequently he came into contact with the brothers John and Charles Wesley, and in 1760 became vicar of Madeley. John Wesley, founder of the Methodist church, spent most of his life after 1742 travelling England, preaching, and visiting religious societies. He frequently visited Madeley after Fletcher's arrival there in 1760. The first of the extracts from his journal refers to his first visit to Madeley in 1764. The second mentions the meeting house which Fletcher erected at Madeley Wood, which still stands, and also describes the preparations for the erection of the Iron Bridge, the parts of which were apparently lying on the banks of the Severn at the time of Wesley's visit. The third is a reminder that roads in Shropshire in the 18th century were as bad as in any other part of England.

Source: *The Journal of John Wesley,* ed. N. Curnock, 1938, Vol. V, p. 87, Vol. VI, pp. 225–6, 345.

21st July 1764.

I rode to Billbrook near Wolverhampton, and preached between two and three. Thence went on to Madeley, an exceeding pleasant village, encompassed with trees and hills. It was a great comfort to me to converse once more with a Methodist of the old Stamp, denying himself, taking up his cross, and resolved to be 'altogether a Christian'.

22nd July 1764 (Sunday).

At ten Mr. Fletcher read prayers, and I preached on these works in the Gospel. 'I am the Good Shepherd, the Good Shepherd layeth down his life for the sheep.' The church would nothing near contain the congregation, but a window near the pulpit being taken down, those who could not come in stood in the churchyard and I believe all could hear. The congregation, they said, used to be much smaller in the afternoon than in the morning, but I would not discern the least difference, either in number or seriousness. I found employment enough for the intermediate hours in

6. '. . . *the new house which Mr. Fletcher has built in Madeley Wood'* (John Wesley, 1779)
The chapel erected for John Fletcher in Madeley Wood in 1776, later the Madeley Wood Methodist School
Photo: The Author

7. '. . . *The church would nothing near contain the congregation . . . those who could not come in stood in the churchyard. . . .*' (John Wesley, 1764)
Madeley Church and Vicarage as they stood in Mr. Fletcher's time (G. Swinney)
Salop County Record Office

praying with various companies who hung about the house, insatiably hungering and thirsting after the Good Word.

* * * * * * *

8. '. . . a Methodist of the old stamp, denying himself, taking up his cross, and resolved to be 'altogether a Christian'. . . .' (John Wesley, 1764)

John Fletcher (Anon)

From an original in the John Fletcher School, Madeley, Telford, copied by courtesy of the headmaster

Thursday 25th March 1779. Preached in the new house which Mr. Fletcher has built in Madeley Wood. The people here exactly resemble those at Kingswood; only they are more simple and teachable. But, for want of discipline, the immense pains which he has taken with them has not done the good which might have been expected. I preached at Shrewsbury in the evening, and on Friday 26 about noon in the assembly room at Broseley . . . We walked from thence to Coalbrookdale and took a view of the Bridge which is shortly to be thrown over the Severn. It is one arch, a hundred feet broad, 52 high and 18 wide; all cast iron, weighing many hundred tons. I doubt whether the Colossus at Rhodes weighed much more.

* * * * * * *

Saturday 23rd March 1782.

It was with a good deal of difficulty we got to Bridgnorth (from Kidderminster); much of the road being blocked up with snow. In the afternoon we had another kind of difficulty, the roads were so rough and so deep that we were in danger every now and then of leaving our wheels behind us. But, by adding two horses to my own, at length we got safety to Madeley.

VI

Joseph Banks (1743–1820), later naturalist with Captain Cook on the voyage of the 'Endeavour', baronet, Privy Councillor and President of the Royal Society, set off in 1767 on a tour of England and Wales on which he kept a detailed journal. He approached the Shropshire coalfield from Stafford, and saw first Early Gower's limeworks and canal (later called the Donnington Wood Canal) which had recently been completed. His account of the ironworks of the Coalbrookdale Company is of particular interest for its pithy description of Richard Reynolds, and for the information it reveals about the experiments with the use of coke to make wrought iron at the Coalbrookdale forges, which were initiated, though Banks does not say so, by the Cranage brothers. The description of the Coalbrookdale Company's railways is also valuable, particularly because it confirms other sources in showing that in 1767 the company were beginning to use iron upper parts on two-level rails. This is generally acknowledged to have been the first use of iron rails. In this extract the original spelling and punctuation are retained.

Source: *The Journal of Joseph Banks* (1767). Original in the Library of the University of Cambridge, MS. Add 6294, reproduced under the title 'Joseph Bank and West Midland Industry', edited by S. R. Broadbridge in *Staffordshire Industrial Archaeology Society Journal*, Vol. 2, 1971, pp. 1-20.

9-10 December 1767.

Return tonight to Bishton in the Morning set out for Lilleshall near Newport Shropshire in the way pass through Stafford & on the street way get there at night & meet the two Mr. Gilberts Went today to see Ld Gowers lime Kilns from which a Large tract of Countrey is supplyd the limestone here is worked under soil a great way & large quantity of Earth & in some places Gretstone taken from it but when this is done many strata of Lime are discovered Containing almost all sorts from the snuff colourd which setts well under water but is not rich Enough for Land to the white which is Best for the Land but Little worth for building . . . From hence went to the navigation which Lord Gower has made for five miles (upon the same principle as the duke of Bridgewaters) for the conveniency of his Coal and Lime with Both which it Communicates & carries them to the turnpike roadside . . .

. . . Went to see Lord Gowers Collierys at Donington wood went into several of the coals which are here workd by Long work which is done thus after their pitts are sunk & ends properly driven they begin to work upon the face of the Coal taking all before them still as they Go throwing their slack behind to support their roof & taking away their Pillars . . .

. . . In one Pit in what is Calld the Donington wood Coal they have a horse who draws for them he is just 10 hands & does them a vast deal of Business living constantly in a little nook cut in the rock just by the pit bottom . . .

. . . Between these Bedds of Coal Lay Bedds of Iron stone many of them of very Excellent Qualities from whence the Quakers Company make their famous Cast metal in Coalbrookdale.

12 December 1767.

Came today through exceeding bad roads to Watling Street upon the Famous roman Road of that name Here I resolvd to stay some time to view carefully the Famous Iron works in this neighbourhood belonging to the Quakers Company . . .

. . . These works are situate between the Severn & the Great turnpike road between which Points they have a rail way Layd for the Convenience of their waggons their Cheif Erections are at three different Places Ketley Horsehay & Coalbrookdale in which they work 7 furnaces & a Forge & turn out a vast Quantity of Iron Mr. Reynolds a Quaker who seemd Particularly Careful of his Speech the Cheif manager told me a great deal more than 100 tons a week I should think more than 150 as their Furnaces I am told have yeilded as much as 30 & are seldom under twenty.

First then Ketley is Situate Just by the turnpike road side here there are three Furnaces which are supplyd with water by two Fire Engines The Largest of which is 68 inches Cylinder The Furnaces are Each of them 12 feet wide & about 31 in hight in the Form of a double Cone blunt at Each End here I saw a Cast of Piggs . . .From hence to Horse hay is two miles here are two furnaces which are supplyd with water by one fire Engine for tho there are two here yet only one works the other standing by to releive it in case of accidents. These five Furnaces are Employd intirely in Casting of Piggs a great Part of which go to the Forge to be made malleable Iron tho some are melted again in air furnaces for castings.

To coalbrookdale is from hence two miles here are two more Furnaces Employd intirely in the casting way which Probably Cast Greater Quantities & better metal than any other in the Kingdom here all Large Casting work is done in the Greatest Perfection they often cast Cylinders for fire Engines as Large as 72 inches diameter & have Cast one as high as 75 I should have thought myself extremely fortunate to have seen any of Their Large ware Cast but was Forcd to content myself with a 90 Gallon Pot the Largest they then had moulded The moulds for these & all smaller Potts are made of sand and charcole dust moulded in a wooden Frame into these they Pour the melted Iron From Ladles made of Iron & covered with Clay to Preserve them from melting as soon as the mould is Filld before the Iron is Compleatly set The air that was Contained in the hollw of the mould rarified by Extreme heat seeks for vent causing a report sometimes as Loud as a pistol but without doing the Least damage . . .

. . . having Traced the Iron through the Furnace we will attend it to the Forge where it is to be made into malleable Iron of these the Company have but one at the dale they selling much Iron in Piggs & having one or more besides at Bridgenorth in this however Iron is made in a new manner

9. *'Mr. Reynolds, A Quaker who seemed particularly careful of his speech. . . .' (Joseph Banks, 1767)*
Richard Reynolds (W. Jobday and S. Bellin

From 'Letters of Richard Reynolds, with a Memoir of his Life' by H. M. Rathbone, 1852

for which they have lately got a Patent it is done intirely with Coaks by this method two Air Furnaces are Constructed by which is mean small ones little Bigger than Large Ovens made of one single arch on one side of which is a grate to make a large Fire on the other a chimney to draw that fire so that Flame beating very strong across the intermediate space Causes an intense heat there into which the Metal is Put in the First of these a fire is made Just sufficient to melt the Piggs which are put into it which as soon as they are in Fusion or scarce advanced quite so far are taken out from thence much in the appearance of half vitrified Cinders they are then removed into the other where as intense a fire as Possible is made here they come to nature as the Forge men term it that is the metal Casts off the dross & runns together in a state fit to be immediately put under the Hammer where by six or seven strokes it is made into an octagonal Bar very rough but fit after this to be Drawn out into Barrs by a very moderate heat . . .

. . . The Iron made by this method is just as good in its Qualities as that made with Charcoal but there is a Large waste of it in the intense heat of the Second Furnace which makes their Invention not near so profitable as was expected . . .

10. '. . . *their railway . . . the most extensive one I believe in this Part of the Kingdom*
& the waggons upon it the Best constructed. . . .' (Joseph Banks, 1767)

A Sketch of a Coalbrookdale Company railway waggon, 1796

Salop County Record Office, Labouchere Collection. Reproduced by kind permission of Lady
Labouchere

. . . I must now say a word or two of their rail way as it is the most extensive
one I believe in this Part of the Kingdome & the waggons upon it the Best
constructed . . . it is made with two Frames the side timbers of Each 4 inches
square those of the Bottom Frame 9 Joind together by Cross Timbers
calld Sleepers which stand about 5 in two yards & Keep the side timbers
steady to support the uppon ones which are pinnd Lengthways upon them
with wooden Pinns these are made of the Firmest heart of Oak that Can
be Got & even that wears out very soon by the immense weights of the
Waggons so much that they have began at the dale to make the upper barrs
of Cast Iron & have thought of Continuing it all their ways.

The waggons themselves are made prodigiously strong their lengh about
10 feet Breadth 4 the weight of Each of them about 22 hundred and
axletrees are Cast Iron & move with the wheels which are Cast Iron likewise
the inner Edge of them overhanging about an inch to Keep them upon the
ways the proper Load of one of them is 2½ tons but they will sometimes
carry 4 nay 5 tons with them in which cases they draw with five horses tho
their Proper number is only three they have many hills in the road some of
them steep these they go by this Contrivance they have a peice of wood
cut in the segment of a circle Calld a Break to fit Each wheel these are
fastend together by Chains one End of which fastend to a staple before the
forewheel the middle Passes under a roller between the wheels & the other

28

End hooks upon the End of a pole 12 feet long Calld the Jig pole which rests in a staple fastend on the hind Part of the Carriage & acting as a lever is directed by the hand of the driver to Confine the breaks Close to the wheels causing just as much Friction as is necessary to make the waggon go at a proper degree of Slowness in case an accident should happen notwithstanding this caution which Can arise from nothing but the Carelessness of the driver there are peices of wood set upon pins which are Easily swung across the road digonaly (catch points) these catch the wheels from their proper tracks & immediately carrey the Carriage against a Little sloping Bank made for the purpose where it immediately stops.

11. '. . . the furnaces, forges, &c. with the vast bellows that give those roaring blasts which make the whole edifice horridly sublime. . . .' (Arthur Young, 1776)

Morning View of Coalbrookdale (William Williams, 1777)

Clive House Museum, Shrewsbury

12. '. . . a winding glen between two immense hills which break into various forms, and all thickly covered with wood, forming the most beautiful sheets of hanging wood . . . too beautiful to be much in unison with that variety of horrors art has spread at the bottom. . . .' (Arthur Young, 1776)

Afternoon View of Coalbrookdale (William Williams, 1777)

Clive House Museum, Shrewsbury

VII

Arthur Young (1741–1820), agricultural journalist, and later secretary to the Board of Agriculture, was one of the most observant of late 18th-century visitors to Coalbrookdale, and one of the most persistent in his enquiries. His account of the district is as remarkable for the detailed information which he collected on such subjects as wages, as it is for his fine descriptive writing. Abraham Darby III's slitting mills which he saw under erection were situated between the upper and lower forges at Coalbrookdale. When Young wrote that there were five furnaces in the Dale, he meant in the Severn Gorge, then often called 'Coalbrookdale'. There were two at Coalbrookdale itself, two at Madeley Wood and one at the Calcutts. John Wilkinson's boring machine was at his Willey ironworks and not at Posenhall.

Source: Arthur Young, *Tours in England and Wales* (L.S.E. reprint, 1932), pp. 145–153.

June 13th, 1776.
Dined [at Shiffnell] and having recommendations from Mr. Harries, of Cruckton, into the neighbourhood of Colebrook Dale, famous for its iron works. Crossed the Severn at the ferry at Lincoln Hill, in the midst of a most noble scenery of exceeding bold mountainous tracts, with that river rolling at the bottom. The opposite shore is one immense steep of hanging wood, which has the finest effect imaginable. Mounted through that wood, thickly scattered with cottages, the inhabitants busily employed in the vast works of various kinds carried on in this neighbourhood. One circumstance I remarked which gave me much pleasure. There was not a single cottage in which a fine hog did not seem to make a part of every family; not a door without a stone trough with the pig eating his supper, in company with the children at the same business playful about the threshold. It was a sight which shewed that chearfulness and plenty crowned the board of the humble but happy inhabitants of this romantic spot.
This neighbourhood is uncommonly full of manufactures, among which the principal are the potteries, pipe makers, colliers and iron works. In the potteries which are only for course mugs, pots etc. the men earn 8s. to 10s. a week. Boys 3d. to 9d. a day, and girls 3d. and 4d. In the pipe manufactory, the men earn 10s. 6d. a week, the women 3s. and children 2s. or 3s., there are 3 or 400 hands employed in it. Both these fabrics are exceedingly

13. '. . . it must be the admiration, as it is one of the wonders, of the world'. (Lord Torrington, 1784)

View of the Cast Iron Bridge near Coalbrook Dale (Michael Angelo Rooker and William Ellis, 1782)

Ironbridge Gorge Museum Trust

flourishing; great numbers of blue tiles are also burnt here, and sent by the Severn to a distance.

Walked by Benthal hall to a steep over the river called Benthal Edge. It is a very fine woody bank which rises very steep from the Severn; you look down an immense declivity on a beautiful winding valley two miles over, cut into rich enclosures, and broken by tufts of wood, the steep on which you stand waving from the right line exhibits the noblest slopes of hanging wood; in one place forming a fine round hill covered with wood, called Tick Wood. In front the Wrekin, three miles off, its sides cut by inclosures three parts up, and along the vale the river meanders to Shrewsbury. Further to the right at a spot called Agar's Spout, a most romantic view down a steep slope of wood with the Severn coming into a very bold reach full against it, winding away to the town in a most bending fanciful course.

Crossing the ferry where Mr. Darby has undertaken to build a bridge of one arch of 120 feet, of cast iron, I passed to his works up Coebrook Dale. The Waggon ways that lead down to the river instead of wood are laid with cast iron; and those made for the limestone waggons on the steep hill are so contrived that the loaded waggon winds up the empty one on a different road. Pass his new slitting mills, which are not finished, but the immense wheels 20 feet diameter of cast iron were there, and appear wonderful.

32

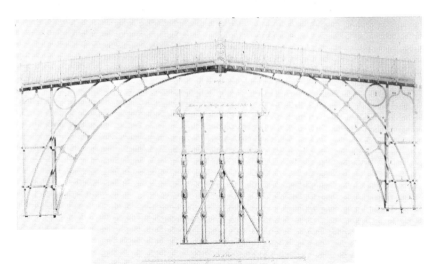

14. '... *of the iron bridge over the Severn ... what shall I say? ...*' (Lord Torrington, 1784)

Elevation and Ribs of the Iron Bridge Cast at Coalbrookdale (William Ellis, 1782)

Ironbridge Gorge Museum Trust

Viewed the furnaces, forges, etc. with the vast bellows that give those roaring blasts, which make the whole edifice horribly sublime. These works are suppose to be the greatest in England. The whole process is here gone through from digging the iron stone to making it into cannons, pipes, cylinders, etc. etc. All the iron used is raised in the neighbouring hills, and the coal dug likewise, which is char'd, an invention which must have been of the greatest consequence after the quantity of cord wood in the kingdom declined. Mr. Darby in his works employs near 1000 people, including colliers. There are 5 furnaces in the Dale, and 2 of them are his: the next considerable proprietor is Mr. Wilkinson, whose machine for boring cannon from the solid cast is at Posenail, and very curious.

The colliers earn 20d. a day, those who get limestone 1s. 4d. the founderers 8s. to 10s. 6d. a week. Boys of 14 earn 1s. a day at drawing coal baskets in the pits. The coal mines are from 20 yards to 120 deep, and the coal in general dips to the south east. There may be about 1000 acres of coal on the Benthal side of the river, and 2000 on the Dale side.

These iron works are in a very flourishing situation, rising rather than the contrary. Colebrook Dale itself is a very romantic spot, it is a winding glen between two immense hills which break into various forms, and all thickly covered with wood, forming the most beautiful sheets of hanging wood. Indeed too beautiful to be much in unison with that variety of horrors art has spread at the bottom: the noise of the forges, mills, &c. with all their vast machinery, the flames bursting from the furnaces with the burning of the coal and the smoak of the lime kilns, are altogether sublime, and would unite well with craggy and bare rocks, like St. Vincent's at Bristol.

33

VIII

John Byng, later fifth Viscount Torrington, was one of the most inveterate of late 18th-century travellers. Born in 1743, he spent many years as an army officer, and on his retirement, took up a somewhat boring post in the Inland Revenue at Somerset House. During breaks from his work, he embarked on long tours of England and Wales. Byng's account of Coalbrookdale is the only source to mention a link between the county authorities and the building of the Ironbridge, and it is probably that this is a garbled and rather inaccurate story, since the minute book of the proprietors of the bridge records no such connection. 'Mr. Bank's Iron furnace' was at the Benthall ironworks. The porcelain manufactury mentioned by Torrington was that founded at Caughley by Thomas Turner which came into production in 1775.

Source: *The Torrington Diaries,* ed. C. Bruyn Andrews, 1934, Vol. I, pp. 283-84.

Tuesday July 20, 1784.

This is the land of bridges; for those of Shrewsbury, Atcham and Berwick are all new and magnificent.

We continued a quiet pleasant good road for some miles round the base of the famed Wrekin Hill, to the village of Leighton, the beginning of the charming Coalbrook-Dale. Thence to Bildewas, where on the opposite shore, stands the noble remains of Bildewas Abbey; which are more perfect than most I had seen, have been on of large scale, and are sweetly situated. The print engrav'd by Buck, 50 years ago shews this ruin in a more entire state, than the smaller print, engrav'd from Grose's drawings, does; and proves that these old buildings are generally deem'd nuisances, which cannot be too soon pull'd down to mend highways, and repair pig styes . . .

On the east side is a gentleman's garden, (whose house has been built from the delapidations of the abbey,) in which there seem'd to be some excellent fruit. At one of the windows of this house there sat a female, who appear'd to have a face, not at all in ruins. All this vale is a most sumptuous garden, so water'd, so wooded, and so studded with good houses. The village of Madeley, comprehending hundreds of detached houses, with the river, woods, rocks, shipping, &c., &c., reminded me of the drawings of a Chinese town, as the same indiscriminate jumble of beauties. But of the iron bridge over the Severn, which we cross'd, and where we stop'd for half an hour, what shall I say? That it must be the admiration, as it is one of the wonders, of the world. It was cast in the year 1778; the arch is 100 feet wide, and 55 feet from the top of the water, and the whole length is 100 yards: the county agreed with the founder to finish it for 6000£; and have, meanly, made him suffer for his noble undertaking. After this survey; we entered Mr. Bank's iron furnace, (on the hillside) and were, most civilly, shewe'd by him all the astonishing progress of such (hellish hot) manufactories: he employes about 700 workmen, & said there were 7 other neighbouring furnaces of the same size; judge then of the flourishing state of this branch of trade, and how it must enrich this vicinage and the kingdom. Every cart belonging to this trade is made if iron, and even the ruts of the road are shod with iron.

Closely adjoining to these works is the town of Broseley, which bears all the marks of content, increase, and riches, not owing only to the iron business, but to a most flourishing pottery and porcelain manufactory.

The whole hill is a mine of coals, and people do not go ten yards for their coals. The face of the country is charming and so it continues by the village of Linley to Bridgnorth.

IX

*Carlo Castone della Torre di Renzionico Comasco was an Italian aristocrat
who visited England in 1787, although it was not until 1824 that the journal
of his tour was published in Venice. His description of Coalbrookdale shows
well how unusual and how awe-inspiring an ironworks could seem in the
late 18th century. The 'fountain of liquid pitch' which Comasco mentions
was the Coalport tar tunnel, the digging of which began in 1786.*

Source: *Viaggio in Einhilterra di Carlo Castone della Torre di Renzionico
   Comasco* (Venice 1824), reprinted and translated in *Salopian Shreds
   and Patches,* 1890, p. 337.

The approach to Coalbrookdale appeared to be a veritable descent to the
infernal regions. A dense column of smoke rose from the earth; volumes of
steam were ejected from fire engines; a blacker cloud issued from a tower in
which was a forge; and smoke arose from a mountain of burning coals which
burst out into turbid flames. In the midst of this gloom I descended towards
the Severn, which runs slowly between two high mountains, and after leaving
which passes under a bridge constructed entirely of iron. It appeared as a
gate of mystery, and night already falling, added to the impressiveness of
the scene, which could only be compared to the regions so powerfully
described by Virgil. I went the same night, following the lurid splendour of
the lighted furnaces, to an adjacent fire engine, and saw the solid ironstone
fused into a liquid. The machines were activated by means of various wheels.
The noise was so great in the long tube which was joined to the furnace that
it could easily be imagined the hissing of the irate furies. The stream of white
hot liquid appeared as the lava of Vesuvius.
On the following morning I considered the construction of the Iron Bridge
very carefully . . . On the Severn may be seen various oval boats constructed
of flexible willow boughs and covered on the outside with horsehide. These
in the language of the country are called *corracles.* The boats were in use in
Britain at the time of the invasion of Julius Caesar, and are even now still
used on the Severn and in various places in Wales where the Celtic language
exists . . .
I also desired to see the fountain of liquid pitch discovered a few months ago
in digging a coal mine. I entered the large cavern which led to it. The vault is
entirely of brickwork, and so appears in great part. At length we arrived at
the rock whence emerges the pitchy torrent in such copiousness that five or

six barrels are filled with it every day. The workmen who gather the pitch, are, of a truth, like the imps described by Dante in his Inferno as gathering with a hook the souls of the damned into a lake of pitch—so horribly disfigured and begrimed are they.

15. '. . . *it appeared as a gate of mystery*' (Carlo Castone della Torre di Renzionico Comasco, 1787)
A View of the Iron Bridge, taken from the Madeley side of the River Severn (James Fittler, 1787)
Ironbridge Gorge Museum Trust

X

Joseph Plymley, archdeacon of Ludlow, was a man of many and varied interests. He was author of 'A General View of the Agriculture of Shropshire', first published in 1803, and ten years earlier compiled a very detailed survey of the social, economic and religious life of those parts of Shropshire within the diocese of Hereford. The original survey is now lost, but fortunately a 19th-century copy with some later additions survives in the British Museum. It is possible here to include only a few items on the parishes in the Severn Gorge from this most valuable source. Plymley gives valuable early evidence and provides interesting comments on the social effects of the high incomes of colliers and ironworkers in Shropshire, his survey is the only source apart from Lord Dundonald's own papers to mention that Dundonald had tar ovens at the Benthall ironworks as well as at the Calcutts, and he makes some interesting remarks about religion in Madeley after the time of John Fletcher.

Source: British Museum Add. MSS. 21018.

Barrow.

A small village on the turnpike road from Wenlock to Bridgnorth . . . 117 houses . . . At Caughley there is a Manufacture of China which employs 100 hands—it is called Shropshire China and is in great esteem . . . A common labourer gets 1/- per day and meat and drink from occasional employers and 10d a day with meat and drink when in constant employ. The men at the china and some other employ obtain much higher wages and several of them belong to benefit clubs at Broseley, Wenlock and elsewhere.

Benthall.

A district of scattered houses in the Franchise of Wenlock . . . 126 houses, numerous shops, warehouses, carthouses, buildings and sheds for miners, limeburners, brickmakers, potters, wharfage, furnaces, foundry offices, boring mill, smithy, stables, barns &c. About 1784 Lord Dundonald erected at this place and at Broseley a number of kilns or stoves for the purpose of extracting Tar from coals, which are still kept working. The following process is used. The stoves are supplied at the bottom with ignited coals, the smoke of which is conveyed by horizontal tubes into a large Funnel erected with brickwork supported upon arches and covered over with a shallow sheet of water, the smoke being condensed by the coolness of the water falls to the bottom of the Funnel in the consistence of tar, which tar is conveyed by pipes into a Receiver whence it is pumped up into a large boiler and is kept there in a heated state till it forms into pitch—the volatile parts which arise during this infusion are again condensed into an oil used for varnish and in the art of jappaning. At ordinary work labourers obtain 16d per day and at the furnace the ordinary workmen have 1s 6d a day.

Broseley.

The least able labourer earns 10s a week at common work in husbandry, and 20s–30s per week in the ironworks . . .

The small children in the parish can earn something in addition to the parents' gains, so that here is ample maintenance for the labourers, but it is generally spent in an improper manner, much of their wages is spent at the alehouse and good living at home is preferred to cleanliness and neatness, either in the person of the people, their clothing, houses or gardens. There are scarcely any instances of a collier or mechanic saving money, otherwise than by contributing to Clubs or Benefit Societies, of which there are six in the parish consisting of about a hundred persons each.

Madeley.

Lincoln Hill . . . a lime work . . . and the more cultivable parts are planted by Mr. Reynolds with shrubs and fir trees, with gravel walks through them, and adorned with temples and other ornamental buildings with iron pillars, rustic seats, and other accommodation, all of which he had dedicated to public use . . . Labourers get 9s a week with 10s in summer from the farmers, and 11s a week with 12s in summer at the furnaces, where some earn as much as 40s per week, but yet it does not appear that these high wages produce more comfort or advantage than at other places—there are 24 ale houses and this additional pay is most spent at these places. These labourers are prone to the indulgences of dainty living, having a pride in buying dear and rare articles at Market for a Sunday dinner or so, tho' they fare harder during the remainder of the week, and there is little attention paid by any of these people to home comforts, neatness of house or garden, or cleanliness of apparel; nothing indeed, seems so difficult as telling whether high or low wages are best for the poor themselves, but the case may be improved by a more general system of Education . . .

The late Mr. de la Flechère, a native of Switzerland, was vicar of the Church for a good length of time, a person of great piety and greatly esteemed by his parishioners. His tomb is covered with a plate of iron . . . sermons given at least twice a week on the evenings of working days in rooms appropriate for that purpose in Coalbrookdale, that being the most populous part of the parish, and at a considerable distance from the church. This custom originated in the time of Mr. de la Flechère, whose zeal for the propagation of Christianity was much adorned by his charity and benevolence. He was a

39

friend of the late Mr. Wesley's. The people are much attached to their evening preachings, and the Quakers who are people of the principal influence here, encourage it very much, perceiving the good effects it has upon the workmen—the persons who attend these meetings frequent the church on Sundays . . . Secretaries in this parish, are, in fact, but few, for though many would be demoninated Methodists, they frequent the church. The Quakers are more considerable in point of property than in numbers, they are liberal in their opinions and do much good.

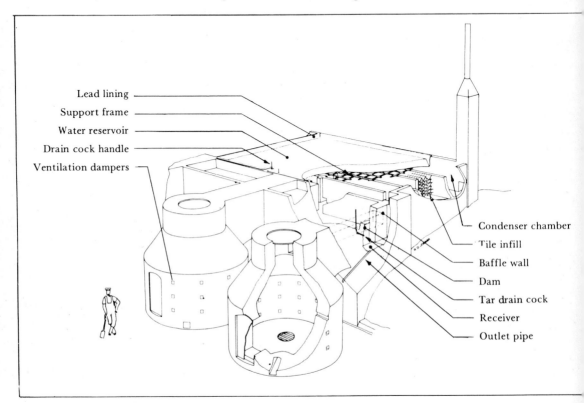

Lead lining
Support frame
Water reservoir
Drain cock handle
Ventilation dampers

Condenser chamber
Tile infill
Baffle wall
Dam
Tar drain cock
Receiver
Outlet pipe

16.　'. . . *a number of kilns or stoves for the purpose of extracting Tar from coals. . . .'* (Joseph Plymley, 1793)

Lord Dundonald's tar and coke kilns at the Calcutts ironworks

A reconstruction of the Calcutts Tar Kilns taken from a plan in the Dundonald Collection, Scottish Record Office, reproduced by permission of the Rt. Hon. Earl of Dundonald. Re-drawn by the late Derek Jobber

XI

Katherine Plymley was the sister of Joseph Plymley (see previous Extract) and lived with him at Longnor on the Shrewsbury–Ludlow road. Her journals which are preserved in the Shropshire Record Office are a most valuable source for the social history of the late 18th- and early-19th-centuries. She was a shrewd and perceptive woman, adept at assessing the personalities of the famous who came to see her brother, who included such diverse people as Thomas Telford, Thomas Clarkson, the philanthropist, and Robert Townson, the traveller and journalist (see Extract XVI). Her account of Coalbrookdale is of interest since it was written from a non-technical viewpoint, and her remarks on Lincoln Hill, its landscaped walks and its limestone mines are particularly valuable.

Source: The Diary of Katherine Plymley, Shropshire Record Office 567 Vol. 27.

June 4th 1794.
(An excursion to Coalbrookdale while Miss Panton was with us during the last month) We dined with my Aunt Flint at Eyton . . . Got to the Iron Bridge in late in the evening, walked through part of the walks planted by

17. ‘. . . no caverns or made grottoes that I have seen can bear the least comparison
(Katherine Plymley, 1794)
The Limekiln at Coalbrookdale (J. M. W. Turner, *c.* 1797)
Ironbridge Gorge Museum Trust

Mr. Reynolds, and which he permits the public to enjoy, till we reached the Rotunda placed on Lincoln Hill, the pillars of it are cast iron, from hence we had a fine view of the Dale by night. The numerous fires have a fine effect not only those in the Dale but several other works towards Broseley, Madeley, &c. The next morning after a delightful walk through other plantations of Mr. Reynolds's, we reached the Dale and look'd at the works of which though I have before seen them, I am too ignorant to speak; it is wonderful to see the vivid green of the plantations so near the smoke of the works, in the close walks it may be supposed that we are in a rural and retired spot, at convenient distances are placed seats which command views of a romantic country and discover how near we are to busy life; there is something in this contrast very pleasing—What pleases me much is a vast cavern of limestone which they work under Lincoln Hill, as they take out the stone they leave massy pillars of it for support, they are formed into grand rude arches, no caverns or made grottoes that I have seen can bear the least comparison with it—what is striking is that it is seen by the light of day let in through some of the outward arches—there is light sufficient to look through these fine caverns and yet gloom sufficient to accord with the scene.

XII

Samuel Ireland, the engraver, was responsible for the plates in Thomas Harral's 'Picturesque Views of the Severn', in which the extract which follows is quoted. Ireland's visit to Coalbrookdale was probably some time in the 1790s, for he died in 1800. His description is one of the best we have of operations at an ironworks in this period.

Source: Thomas Harrall, *Picturesque Views of the Severn,* Vol. I, 1824, p. 229.

The immense furnace stood in the centre of a large area walled around, communicating with each side of which was a colossal pair of bellows, whose alternate blasts, with a noise like the incessant roaring of heavy ordnance, excited an intense heat, which had to be kept up night and day, for a considerable time to separate the metal from the stone, and to reduce it into a state of fusion. The aperture whence the fused iron was to flow was guarded only by some clay and sand, constantly kept moist by the application of water. Preparatory to the opening of the furnace, a channel of damp sand was formed, from its mouth to a large circular basin of the same material, into which, on its liberation, the burning fluid impetuously rushed. On a wide surrounding space, were numerous moulds, in sand, for the fronts of stoves and other articles. Into these the fluid iron was poured from ladles with long handles, carried by athletic workmen, who filled these utensils from the great circular reservoir. So intense was the heat of the metal, that the moment the ladles, though very thick and ponderous, were dipped into it, they became red hot, far above the bowl. Indeed, were it not that the labourers were supplied with gloves, so constructed as to protect them from the violence of the heat, even at the upper parts of the ladle hafts, it would be impossible for them to perform their work.

XIII

Charles Hatchett (1766–1847) was the son of a coachmaker who in 1790 went to Russia with a coach made by his father for Catherine the Great. He was interested in geology and chemistry, and helped to arrange the collection of minerals in the British Museum. In 1796 he embarked on a tour which took him from Cornwall to the north of England. His main interests were in mining and minerals, but his description of the Ironbridge Gorge includes detailed accounts of the operation of the blast furnaces at Coalbrookdale (which can be compared with that of Samuel Ireland), of the boring shops at the Calcutts ironworks, and of the Coalport Tar Tunnel, into which Hatchett ventured further than most visitors. Hatchett was the first tourist to leave an account of the Coalport porcelain factory set up by John Rose and Edward Blakeway shortly before the time of his visit.

Source: *The Hatchett Diary,* ed. A. Raistrick, ed. 1967, pp. 57-60.

Wednesday June 1st 1796.

Coal Brook Dale or at least the principal Iron Foundery is situated on the Northern side of the Severn about one Mile from the Banks but on each side of the river are a great number of houses in different large groups which all called by different names—these are inhabited chiefly by People more or less concerned in the different Iron and Coal works which are here very numerous. The Banks of the Severn on either side are flanked by Mountains beautifully wooded and the appearance is uncommonly Picturesque and Romantic. The River near the Iron Bridge runs from about NW to SE it is not very broad but rapid.

This place has the remarkable advantage of finding in the mountains on the banks of the river Iron Ore, Coal and (in the neighbourhood) Lime Stone so that Nature has here supplied every requisite material for Smelting the ores of Iron. In the morning after Breakfast we went to see the Principal Iron Foundery called the Dale Works the situation of which I have mentioned—these belong to a Quaker Family of the name of Darby which by marriage is connected with another Quaker family of the name of Reynolds which is in possession of most of the other great works, and I was informed by the old Quaker who shewed us the works that in the district belonging to these two families between 30 and 40,000 souls are supported either by working in the Founderies or in the Iron & Coal Mines. The Furnaces of these works are about 30 feet high and the Blast is

44

18. '... *the remainder of the Iron is poured into another channel formed in sand which has a number of shorter running laterally from it, thus the long one is called the Sow and the short ones the Pigs.* ...' (Charles Hatchett, 1796)

The Inside of a Smelting House, at Broseley Shropshire (William Lowry, *c.* 1788)
Ironbridge Gorge Museum Trust

produced by large cylinders instead of bellows. The Furnace is charged at the top with Ore (which has been roasted) mingled with Lime Stone for the fluxing the fuel is Coak which they make upon the spot by partially charring or burning the Pit coal covered with Earth and Ashes. They tap the Furnace twice in the course of a Day and each time cast between 3 and 4 Tons (20,000 to the Ton) of Iron. The metal is by a channel made in Sand conveyed into a sort of trough of Iron which serves as a reservoir out of which they Ladle it into different Moulds. When all these are filled they raise the back of the Trough by a Crane and Hook so that the remainder of the Iron is poured into another channel formed in sand which has a number of shorter running laterally from it thus the long one is called the Sow and the short ones the Pigs. Some of the Pig Iron is worked under the great hammers in the Forges belonging to this establishment into Bar Iron or into Stamps for Stamping Mills and the rest is melted again for casting vessels and other utensils in an Air Furnace in which the flame is reverberated. The Celebrated Iron Bridge over the Severn was cast in this Foundry and they have made one to be fixed at Bridgewater. They have also begun a third for themselves. After dinner we went to see Mr. Brodies Foundery for cannon (all of 32 Pounders). The Cannon are moulded in 4 pieces which are afterwards joined. The cannon when cast are solid and the weight of two (which is the number cast at each time) is 7 tons 12 cwt. The cannon are then (by a square piece formed at the Breach) fixed in a mortice in the centre of a cogged wheel which is turned by a Steam Engine (7 or 8 are worked at one time) the extra pieces at the Muzzles are then cut off by a hard sharp plate of steel and they are then bored. The borer by an ingenious and simple contrivance is made by weights and a carriage to advance on a rack worked in proportion as it penetrates the Cannon.

45

This foundery of Mr. Brodies is about one mile and a ¼ SE of the Iron Bridge on the SW bank of the River.

Near Mr. Brodies Foundery is a Building erected by Lord Dundonald . . . for the distilling of Pit coal—by this process the Bitumenous part of the coal (which is lost in the usual way of making Coak) is conveyed through long winding chimneys and after being condensed is received in a Recipient.

On the NE Bank of the river nearly opposite to Mr. Brodies but rather farther from the Iron Bridge is a Tunnel cut in the side of a Mountain of whitish Arcillaceous Grit which is about 1040 yds long and into which we penetrated abt 760 yds—in this gallery or tunnel Petroleum is found which drips through the grit into a small rill of water from the top of which it is collected. The lower part of the Sand stone or Grit is penetrated with Petroleum which now sells for 5 guineas the Barrel (36 gallons) part of this is rectified on the spot to make British Oil. This Gallery communicates with a Coal Mine of considerable depth. About 100 yds from this last place is a Porcelain Manufactory lately established. The ware is like that of Worcester and the materials the same.

19. '. . . a Tunnel cut in the side of a Mountain. . . .' (Charles Hatchett, 1796)
The Tar Tunnel, Coalport
Photo: Ironbridge Gorge Museum Trust

The Mountains which form the banks of the Severn at Coalbrookdale are lofty and are sloped rapidly towards the river. A little above the Dale to the NW the mountains open on each side towards a Plain. It is in these Mountains that the iron ore and coal are found in a wonderful abundance. The coal is often found over the Iron Ore but the latter never over the former. The Iron and Coal Mines are often by the side of each other within the distance sometimes of a few yards. The Iron Ore is not rich in quality but this is compensated by the quantity and the ease with which it is obtained. Many of the coal and Iron Mines are entered by lateral Galleries as they call them here—Tunnels. The Tontine or Iron Bridge Inn very excellent. Iron rail roads invented by Mr. John Curr of Sheffield are made here for the coal works also the Inclined Planes. The ropes which move the Corves or Carts on these are worked by a small Steam Engine, first used here now also at Attercliffe Colliery near Sheffield.

46

XIV

On their way back to London after a stay in Shrewsbury in August 1796, the Prince and Princess of Orange, Stadholder William V (1748-1806) and Princess Wilhelmina made a tour of the principal places of interest in the Severn Gorge. 'Mr. Brodie's cannon foundry' was part of the Calcutts iron-works, and 'Coal-park' should read Coalport.

Source: *Salopian Journal,* 24 August 1796.

Their Highnesses the Prince and Princess of Orange, on their return from this town, visited the Dale Company's iron-works, where they were very respectfully received by the company; went by water to see Mr. Brodie's cannon foundry, where they were saluted by firing of cannon, and other tokens of respect; the Prince was highly pleased to see the boring of ten cannons at the same time: And thence proceeded to the china factory at Coal-park, where her Highness bought some pieces of Mr. Rose; and after viewing the Tar Spring, the inclined plane &c., returned to the Tontine Inn about three o'clock, where their Highnesses dined, and at half past four set out for Bridgnorth, Kidderminster and Worcester. They were pleased to express great satisfaction at the accommodations and attendance they met with in the Dale and its vicinity.

20. '. . . *Mr. Brodie's cannon foundry, where they were saluted by firing of cannon and other tokens of respect. . . .'* (Salopian Journal, 1796)

An Iron Work, for Casting of Cannon: and a Boreing [sic] Mill, taken from the Madeley side of the River Severn, Shropshire (Wilson Lowry, *c.* 1788)

Ironbridge Gorge Museum Trust

21. '. . . *the china factory at Coal-port, where her highness bought some pieces of Mr. Rose. . . .*'
(Salopian Journal, 1796)

The Coalport China Works (T. Jewitt)

Ironbridge Gorge Museum Trust

22. '. . . *the Tontine Inn . . . where their Highnesses dined. . . .*' (Salopian Journal, 1796)

The Tontine Hotel, Ironbridge, 1975

Photo: The Author

XV

Joshua Gilpin was an American Quaker whose principal business interests were in papermaking. He kept journals on several extended tours of England in the late 18th and early 19th centuries. His account of his visit to Shropshire in 1796 is particularly valuable for the light which it throws on the activities of William Reynolds. Gilpin visited Reynolds's laboratory at Ketley Bank House, heard about his glassworks at Wrockwardine Wood, saw his collection of fossils, and met the artist who was painting his portrait. The pottery he mentions at Coalport was probably that of Rose and Blakeway in which Reynolds had invested heavily. The portrait by Wilson (plate 32) now hangs in the Coalbrookdale Museum.

Source: Joshua Gilpin, Journals and Notebooks, 1790-1801, in the State Archives, Harrisburg, Pennsylvania. Microfilm in University of Birmingham Library.

6 Nov. 1976.

J. Dearman came to Sunniside to breakfast—after breakfast went with him to the other furnace called Horsehay—ab. 2 miles—stopped to view a number of Basaltic columns—they were much larger than the Giants Causeway tho' like them of five sides . . . after seeing them stopt some time at the furnace and went on to Ketley Furnace and works—went first to Joseph Reynolds—saw his wife, sister of J. Dearman of London, went thro' the Ketley works thence to dine with him—after dinner to the inclined plane and in the evening to the Bank, William Reynolds's seat—went thro' his laboratory—saw large collections of Fossills—went to the Quarry picked out a number of fossills from the sandstone chiefly Tropical Plants entirely formed into stone—underneath the sand. Same kind of clay (erroneously called Marl) as at Hanley, mixd in this lies the Iron Stone in Roundish pebbles picked out by women and children—coal mined chiefly under the Marl—several inclined planes at work here in drawing up the iron, coals &c. Returned in the evening.

7th Nov.

Rose at 8 and remained at home till 11 then went again to Meeting—& to dine with Richard Reynolds—in the afternoon walked down the Severn to Coalport met William Reynolds there, several gentlemen with him. This is the port on the Severn where the coal and other production brought down the canals particularly the Shropshire Canal is shipped down the Severn

49

for the country below—above 40,000 tons annually hence—besides a number of vessells loaded who had been waiting since 9 May for want of water to go down . . . Went thro' Mr. Reynolds's Pottery lately established here—makes the yellow ware as good and cheap as Staffordshire, also China very good. Went from hence to the Coal Tar spring—it broke out some years ago by running a level into the hill for Coal, went up the level about 1100 yards—in many places the rock forms the arch—in others 'tis bricked—first intended for a Canal, but since the improvements of railroads and waggons made into a dry tunnel . . .

8th Nov. My Birthday.

Rose at 8—after breakfast walked down to the Office and went with Mark Gilpin Jun. to the Iron Bridge—has a beautiful appearance on both sides—has proved very strong—but is not built with Mathematical truth as the inner arch or rib in the main support of the two parallel ones, being no addition of its strength but much to the weight. Went from the Bridge up the Shifnal road to the hills whence the limestone is dug. The Top of these hills very high. Strata of Limestone and Sandstone alternate. The Limestone procurred into the hill and tremendous caverns formed in which it has been obtained—sent down the hill by the inclined plane. Coals also brought up and some of it burned on the spot. Among the loose earth on the Top of the Hill is found an immense number of shells of almost every kind—but chiefly very small. On the pinnacle of a very point of the hill, Richard Reynolds has erected a round temple called a Rotunda ab. 10 feet diam. Pillars of cast iron hollow. Roof of Lead. The view from here commands all the vale which is beautifully wooded—and with the immense number of works it forms a scene highly picturesque. Came home, dined. In the afternoon walked with J. Dearman up the Severn to Buildwas where the Dale Company are building a new bridge . . .

11th Nov.

Left Shrewsbury at 10 . . . Reached Ketley at 12 . . .
Called on J. Reynolds, went thence to Coal Bank, seat of William Reynolds, saw there Dr. Young,—Wilson a Portrait Painter of Birmingham, John Dearman and his wife. They soon went away. Dined with William Reynolds, Dr. Young and Mr. Wilson, the last employed by R. Crawshaw in painting the chief iron founders in the kingdom—was finishing Mr. Reynolds's, J. Wilkinson and R. Crawshaw. After dinner got a number of the Ironstone fossills, saw a hugh glass bottle containing 70 or 80 gallons made at his glass house—left Coal Bank and returned, stopped at Horsehay works and saw them roll bar iron and heat it. Reached Sunniside about 7 o'clock. Meeting—15 to 20 attended

13th Nov.

Left Sunniside at 2 o'clock. Called at Mark Gilpin's, crossed the Dale and came upon the North side. On rising the hill the view of this beautiful Dale,

23. '*. . . the Iron Bridge . . . has a beautiful appearance . . . has proved very strong. . . .*' (Joshua Gilpin, 1976)

A View of the Cast Iron Bridge over the River Severn at Coalbrookdale in Shropshire (F. Edgecombe, 1768)

Ironbridge Gorge Museum Trust

24. '*. . . went thence to Coal Bank, seat of William Reynolds. . . .*' (Joshua Gilpin, 1796)

Ketley Bank (formerly Coalpit Bank) House, 1975

Photo: The Author

its woods, the small pieces of water, its numerous buildings, scattered everywhere on the sides of the hills and in the bottom of the vale the smoak of the furnaces and the small river of Severn winding thro' and covered with boats and the masts of shipping—the quarries of stone and numerous precipices and declivities formed by them—all together formed a scene of picturesque peace and pleasing beyond description.

25. '. . . *made at his glass house.* . . .' (Joshua Gilpin, 1796)
A Wrockwardine Wood glass jug
Crown copyright, Victoria and Albert Museum

XVI

A letter of December 1795 from William Reynolds, the Shropshire iron-master, to the son of Matthew Boulton of the Soho Manufactory, reveals that Robert Townson, who had studied chemistry with the younger Boulton in Paris, was then staying with Reynolds. In 1796 and again in 1797 Townson stayed with Joseph Plymley and his sister Katherine at Longnor. Townson was a mineralogist and naturalist, who had studied at Gottingen and travelled widely in Eastern Europe. His publications varied from an account of the natural history of the tortoise to a description of his travels in Hungary. Katherine Plymley saw him as a man who always carried 'a hammer for tapping rocks, a tin for insects and a net for butterflies, a portfolio on his back for pressing plants, and a gun in his hand', and thought that he was a man of great ability, although a nuisance to the friends who entertained him. The first paragraph in this extract from his pamphlet on the geology of Shropshire describes the Coalport Tar Tunnel. The 'famous spring' mentioned in the second is the Burning Well at Broseley, a great object of popular curiosity in the early 18th century which had been extinguished by mining operations in the 1750s.

Source: *Tracts and Observations in Natural History and Physiology,* London 1799. *A Sketch of the Mineralogy of Shropshire.*

The so famous spring of mineral tar of pitch exudes from fissures in a sandstone impregnated with it, and lying over a stratum of coal, but from which it is separated by an argillaceous stratum. At this present time it only yields about thirty gallons per week, formerly it yielded near a thousand gallons in one week; and at first, when the level or adit was driving, many barrels were collected in one day. It is supposed that were there a demand for it, a much great quantity could be obtained by driving through fresh fissures. In the upper part of this bituminous sandstone, a great many rounded pieces of coal are imbedded. In the neighbourhood of this tar spring, several springs of salt water have been found, yet none lately of sufficient strength to be worth working. The water which exudes from the flint coal in some works in the parish of Madeley, is likewise salt; and in the adjoining parish of Broseley there was formerly a salt works, where the salt is said to have been made from water taken out of the coal pits, which to this day, are called the Salt House pits. The famous spring which formerly threw out so great a quantity of inflammable air was at Broseley.

In this coal district are the following iron works. In the south is Willey, Broseley, Calcot and Benthall; these are on the south side of the Severn. On the north side of this river is Madeley Wood, Coalbrook Dale, Lightmoor, Horse Hay, Old Park, Snedshill, Ketley and Donnington. These works employ about six thousand hands; and annually about 260,000 tons of coal are raised in this district. It is worth remarking that Coalbrook Dale can justly claim the merit of having, in the beginning of this century, introduced upon a large scale, the use of coaked coal, as a substitute for charcoal, in the making of iron.

XVII

The letters of the admiralty engineer, Simon Goodrich, to Sir Samuel Bentham, inspector-general of navy works, and brother of Jeremy Bentham, the political economist, are preserved in the Science Museum and contain much valuable information about Midlands industries in the late 18th century. In Shropshire Goodrich was not content merely to look at such well-known spots as Coalbrookdale and the Iron Bridge, but penetrated to sites which visitors usually neglected. He went to the Onions family's Snedshill ironworks as well as to Ketley, Coalbrookdale and the Calcutts, to the Wrockwardine Wood inclined plane as well as to Windmill Farm and The Hay. The railway he mentions, built in opposition to the Shropshire Canal, was that which ran from ironworks in the Oakengates area to Sutton Wharf, downstream from Coalport. Perhaps the most intriguing feature of this letter is its revelation that William Reynolds was experimenting with some form of oil engine, using as fuel one of the hydrocarbons produced in Lord Dundonald's tar-making process.

Source: Letters from Simon Goodrich to General Sir Samuel Bentham, Goodrich Collection, Science Museum, South Kensington, London.

Friday 6 Decr. 1799.

I Breakfasted at Watling Street, and proceded from thence back again towards Oaken Gates, at the half way between were Messrs. Reynolds works of Ketley—as I had learnt that Strangers were excluded from these works I went to Mr. Reynolds's house to request permission from himself to walk about them; as I find it generally the best way in these cases to apply to the head at once—unfortunately neither of the Mr. Reynolds's were at home. I then applied to their Foreman at the works, but was answerd that he dared not permit me to inspect them without a line from Mr. Reynolds. I have since been informed that with regard to mechanism there is nothing different in these works from what is to be seen at others, and they are only thus difficult of access upon account of some little variation in the process of making Iron by which means they have the character of producing the best. I did not quite lose my labor, for near the rest of their works I examined a Steam Engine & the means by which its power was transmitted to work a pump situated about 200 yards from it . . .

. . . . I proceeded to Mr. Onions works at Oaken Gates. I applied to young Mr. Onions who was at the works, for leave to walk about them which was

26. '. . . Mr. Onions & Co. . . . had laid down a rail road by the side of the Canal 8 miles *in length and could transport their goods by it down to the River Severn cheaper than by the Canal'* (Simon Goodrich, 1799)

Sutton Wharf, the terminus of the railway from Oakengates to the Severn, 1975

Photo: The Author

readily granted. I here examined 4 Steam Engines, one a single Engine of B & W, of 42 inches diameter, 7 ft. stroke which work's a double blowing cylinder. Another a common atmospherical Steam Engine 50 inches diamr. & 4 Feet stroke which workd a single blowing tub . . . The other 2 Steam Engines workd the forge hammers by means of cranks and Flywheels, one of them was a well constructed common atmospherical engine, the other was similar in appearance but had an air pump and condenser . . . Young Mr. Onions with whom I had much conversation walk'd with me to an inclind'd plane for Boats about a mile to the north of Oaken Gates. I saw a loaded boat taken up and an empty one let down. Mr. Onions & Co. in opposition to the Canal company with whom they had some disagreement had laid down a rail road by the side of the Canal 8 miles in length and could transport their goods by it down to the River Severn cheaper than by the Canal. The original cost of the Rail Road is about 1/10 of the Canal. I return's with Mr. Onions to Oaken gates—in the way saw two Field Engines such as are now generally used for drawing the coals up from the Pits. One of them was a double Engine of B and W small cylinder, about 3 ft. stroke and could work at the rate of 60 Strokes pr. minute. The other was an atmospherical with the Crank under the Cylinder like Mr. Sadlers. Having taken proper directions from Mr. Onions I proceeded towards Colebrook Dale.

In my way thither I stopped at & examined Mr. Botfields works at the Park furnace. I here saw 3 large common Engines, Blowing Tubs and Forge Hammers at work. I also went to Horshay works which are near the Dale Company, but was prevented looking about by a Clerk who said he could not permit me without a line from his superiors. I had learnt that a Mr. Dearman was chief manager of the Dale companys works, & that his house & office was at the Dale. I went, I call'd at the Dale Office. Mr. Dearman was not there but I was informd that he & the Mr. Reynolds's were at the Tontine Inn at the Foot of the Iron Bridge. When I arrivd at the Inn these Gentlemen had been gone away about ½ an hour, it being now dark my excursion was finished for the Day, and I have taken up my abode for tonight at the Tontine Inn.

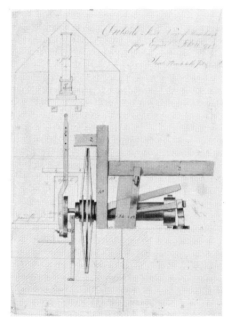

27. '. . . I arriv'd at Horsehay works and saw common Steam Engines, a B & W Steam Engine, a Water Wheel . . . forge hammers, rollers for making plate iron, blast engine with a water regulator and Furnaces all at work. . . .' (Simon Goodrich, 1799)
Outside Front View of Horsehays forge Engine, Feby. 21, 1793 (From the William Reynolds Sketch Book)
Photo: Science Museum, London

Saturday 7th Decr. 1799.

I examined the Iron Bridge as soon as it was daylight. After getting breakfast I proceded towards the Dale Company's Office. Stopt & examined a Boring Mill in my way thither. It was work'd by a water wheel & was then Boring a Cylinder about 2 ft. diamr. the bit made a revolution of ½ minute. When I arriv'd at the Dale office Mr. Dearman was not at home, but after giving some account of myself & of my wishes to (as 'supposed') the next in authority, he gave me permission to see the works and sent a young man with me to conduct me about them . . .

. . . Having sufficiently examine'd these works I requested leave to see their other works at Horsehay about a mile from these & they furnished me with a few lines ordering their Clerks there to shew me them. Between the Dale and Horsehay works is a rail road which is in a bad state owing I conceive to their here using one large Carriage instead of several small ones by which means too great a pressure is brought upon too small a surface, & the consequence is that either the wheels of the carriage or the rails they run upon, tho' both made much stronger than in other cases, are frequently broken, or the railways driven out of their places, or crushed into the ground. I arriv'd at Horsehay works and saw common Steam Engines, a B & W Steam Engine, a Water wheel but not with cast iron shaft, forge hammers, rollers for making plate iron, blast engine with a water regulator and Furnaces all at work.

28. *'I was up by day light and went & examined the Water wheel which was the reverse extreme of Mr. Strutt's large Water wheel at Belper being only one foot wide in the ladle and about 60 ft. diamr.'* (Simon Goodrich, 1799)

The Mill Wheel at Benthall, *c.* 1920

Photo: Ironbridge Gorge Museum

Taking direction from hence I cross'd over the Country to the Shropshire Canal and arriv'd at an inclin'd plane for Boats, call'd the Windmill or Sterchley Incline. Its length was 665 yards and I guess it rose about 4 inches pr. yard, not being able to learn that particular from the men on the spot I proceded about 2 miles farther along the bank of the canal and arrived at another Inclined Plane at Coalport, by which the boats are taken up from, or let down into a Canal close by the side of the River Severn. The length of this Incline was 230 yards & it rose 9 inches in the yard. These two Inclined Planes as well as the one I saw yesterday were exactly upon the same Plan & the same Machinery was used in all . . . A Heslops Steam Engine of 10 or 12 Horses power is . . . used to work the machinery . . .

At the bottom of this last Inclined Plane I crossed in a boat over the Severn & proceeding a little way up the side of the River I arrived at Mr. Brodie's Cannon Foundry. I here examined an extensive apparatus for turning & boring Guns. There was no work of either kind then actually going on, but one of the workmen fully explained the whole to me. I also examined two large atmospherical Steam Engines with a Condenser & Air Pump one of them with a very heavy Fly Wheel worked the boring apparatus the other supplied the blast to the furnace thro' the means of one Cylinder pumping the air into another which had a weighted regulating piston. Close by Mr. Brodie's works was a Manufactory for extracting Tar from Coals belonging to Lord Dundonald, this I next examined and had the whole explained to me by two of the workmen . . . Besides the many useful purposes to which the Oil of Tar is applied, perhaps the attempt made by a man in London to work an engine by exploding small quantities of it may be brought to greater perfection. On the evening that I was at the Public House at Oaken Gates I learnt from the workmen there that a Young Man of the name of Glassbrook was contriving a new kind of Engine at Mr. Reynolds's of Ketley of the effect of which they gave a wonderfull account. Talking over the subject next day with young Mr. Onions, I explained to him a plan I once contrived for working with rarefied air, which he said was precisely the same thing as a model of this Mr. Glassbrook's which he had seen. From this I concluded his plan could produce no beneficial effect. But yet having been informed that the Man was still going on, that something different from Steam Engines was to be produced, being now accidentally informed by the Workmen who were shewing me this Manufactory that Mr. Reynolds had ordered a considerable quantity of oil of Tar, I am led to suspect that being disappointed upon the plan of rarefied air, they are now attempting to produce some mechanical effect with this Oil of Tar.

From the Coal Tar manufactory I proceeded up the side of the river to the Iron Bridge near which I observed an extraordinary water wheel but it being then too dark to examine in properly, I cross'd over the Bridge to the Tontine Inn intending to see it again tomorrow morning before I set off for Wolverhampton.

Sunday 8th December 1799.

I was up by day light and went & examined the Water wheel which was the reverse extreme of Mr. Strutt's large Water wheel at Belper being only one foot wide the ladle and about 60 ft. diamr. A small stream of water from a hill was conducted in a trough & let nearly upon the top of the wheel but was not carried over it as it might have been, so that the wheel was what is termed a Back overshot wheel . . . As the wheel was not at work during either of the times that I saw it and not meeting with persons upon the spot to make the enquiry, I could not learn what kind of work it was used for.

From examining this Water wheel & admiring the beauty & neatness of its appearance, I repassed the Iron Bridge to the Tontine Inn & breakfasted. As there are many plans & drawings of the Iron Bridge extant it is needless for me to describe it. I shall however observe that the Abutments have suffered from the violence of some high floods and the one that has been the longest has been perforated with iron bars clamped at the ends with other flat bars in order to keep the Stones together. The sides of the abutment appear to have been carried up too perpendicularly without a sufficient width of base or buttresses of a proper size to resist the great pressure of high floods. At 11 o'clock I left the Tontine Inn and set off on foot for Wolverhampton. I passed by the Sterchly Inclined Plane, and saw several fixed Steam Engines for the purpose of drawing up Coals out of Pits . . . I stopped at Shifnal & dined, afterwards proceeded on to Wolverhampton where I arrived by 4 o'clock in the afternoon & took up my quarters for the night.

XVIII

Richard Warner (1763–1857) was an Anglican clergyman who published extensive journals of his travels in Great Britain as well as many volumes of sermons and devotional literature. At the time of his tour in 1801 he was curate of St. James's Church, Bath, and from 1809 until 1857 was rector of Great Chalfield, Somerset.

Source: Richard Warner, *A Tour through the Northern Counties of England,* 1802, Vol. II, pp. 182, 185–87.

July 27th 1801.
Wellington . . . surrounded by founderies and in the neighbourhood of iron mines and coal works is rapidly rising to opulence and importance . . . We passed on to Coalbrookdale, through Ketley by the vast founderies of Messrs. Reynolds, and over Ketley Heath, the inexhaustible storehouse of iron ore and coal. But our wonder was still more excited by Coalbrookdale itself, a scene in which the beauties of nature and processes of art are blended together in curious combination. The valley which is here hemmed in by high, rocky banks, finely wooded, would be exceedingly picturesque, were it not for the huge founderies, which, volcano like, send up volumes of smoke into the air, discolouring nature, and robbing the trees of their beauty; and the vast heaps of red hot iron ore and coak that give the bottom 'ever burning with solid fire' more the appearance of Milton's hell than of his paradise. At the extremity of the vale, the celebrated iron bridge, which tho' not so vast as that at Sunderland, is more striking from the singularity of the scenery accompanying it . . .
. . . The great works at the Dale belong to the society called the Coalbrookdale Company; the lesser ones are private speculations. One of the chief proprietors Mr. Reynolds is the landowner of this romantic spot; who, possessing as much liberality as taste, has preserved in a great measure its picturesque beauties, and laid them open to the enjoyment of the public. This he has effected by conducting two walks in the most judicious manner over the brow of the vast ampitheatrical hill that rises above the vale of Severn and commands the opposite banks and a long reach of subsequent country. The first of these conducts to a plain Doric temple, through a thick shade occasionally opening and disclosing the rocky banks on the other side of the Dale; from those bosom the ascending smoke, curling up in vast volumes from the founderies that are unseen, suggests the idea of the

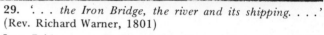

29. '. . . the Iron Bridge, the river and its shipping. . . .'
(Rev. Richard Warner, 1801)

Iron Bridge near Coalbrookdale (Samuel Ireland, *c.* 1795)

Ironbridge Gorge Museum Trust

30. '. . . a curious wheel of a mill is seen, whose circumference is 162 feet, made of cast iron at the adjoining works. . . .' (Rev. Richard Warner, 1801)

The Mill Wheel at Benthall, *c.* 1930

Photo: Ironbridge Gorge Museum

mist arising from the agitation of a cataract; the notion is strengthened by the incessant din of the volcanic operations below. Returning along this path, we crossed the road to the second, which is led along the narrow ridge of an eminence agreeably planted with evergreens, which shut out the immense limestone pits to the left hand, and interrupt the sight of a deep precipice to the right. This walk terminates with a rotunda, a most classical building, placed at the point of the promontory; whence a view of great extent, diversity and curious combination is unfolded. Immediately under the abrupt height on which it stands, yawning caverns disclose themselves, the entrances into the limestone quarries, from whence ever and anon waggons drawn by horses and laden with the produce of the mine are seen to issue; and in their neighbourhood a series of pits stand ready to receive the stone, vomiting smoke and burning flame. Carrying the eye a little further, it takes in the Iron Bridge, the river and its shipping. Beyond this it reposes in distant vales, and upon the fertile meadows of Shropshire; whilst, once more returning to the nearer pasture, it catches that magnificent scenery the bank we had before traversed and its Doric temple, together with the rocks and woods and windings of the dale.

Taking the Bridgnorth road, we passed over the Iron Bridge, and wound up a steep and long hill that repaid us on turning round for the tediousness of its ascent, by a fine view of the Severn, Madeley vale, the great iron works, and the romantic above them; whilst to the left, a cliff lifted itself high above the bottom, scarred into lime quarries, which produced inexhaustible quantities of the coarse stone that is thrown into the furnace with the iron ore as a flux. Under its beetling brow, a curious wheel of a mill is seen, whose circumference is 162 feet, made of cast iron at the adjoining works. The cottages tucked as if by accident on the rocky sides of these heights add much to the singularity of the picture.

XIX

Charles Dibdin (1745–1814), the famous dramatist and song writer, was a friend of the Shropshire landowner and fox-hunter, George Forester, of Willey, and wrote a well-known song in honour of Forester's whipper-in, Tom Moody, who died in 1796. It was probably while visiting Forester about 1787 that Dibdin saw the newly-discovered Tar Tunnel, which he recalled 14 years later. This is one of the most informative sources on the tunnel. Dibdin was one of the few visitors of the Ironbridge Gorge to find the pollution of the air intolerable.

Source: Charles Dibdin, *Observations on a Tour through almost the whole of England and a considerable part of Scotland in a series of Letters*, London, 1801–02, Vol. II, pp. 309–12.

There are mines of copper, lead and iron in Shropshire and many coal pits, one of which was discovered not long ago to contain a stratum of bituminous quality; and indeed is the very place where it is well known tar was extracted from coal; but it has excited very much my wonder that we now hear so little of the tar spring in Coalbrookdale, of which the pitchy opening spoken of above gives us some hint. I saw this tar spring fourteen year ago, and shall now set down my observations on it made at that time, while my imagination was yet warm with this very extraordinary phenomenon. I went in company with a gentleman into the mouth of a bricked arch-way, which reached three-hundred yards; and when we had got about thirty yards, we began to see the tar ooze from the crannies in the rock. It must be understood that from the top of the rock a pit had been sunk, which went to such an immense depth that it would have been very expensive, and indeed almost impracticable to work it. Finding, however, the coals of an admirable quality, it was thought worth while to form the arch-way above described at the foot of the mountain, and as near as possible to the Severn, that the coal might be drawn out in carriages, which mode of getting at them, instead of the usual way, it was thought would be so much more expeditious and convenient, as to make a saving, in a short time, equal to the expence of having formed the arch-way. In the prosecution of this scheme, the tar unexpectedly made its appearance, at first oozing as we have seen it, and afterwards pouring forth in a large body, which fairly flowed into the Severn. The discovery was made known, and the course of the tar as soon as possible diverted by means of iron pipes,

64

31. '. . . *Coalbrookdale wants nothing but Cerberus to give you an idea of the heathen hell. The Severn may pass for the Styx.* . . .' (Charles Dibdin, 1801)

Lateral Mine Shafts beside the Severn (Charles Dibdin)

which were, as far as my recollection guides me, nearly as large as those which convey the water from the New River in London. Large pits were immediately dug, and immense cauldrons sunk. In these the tar was boiled, and became pitch. When I saw the place, there were three springs, one of which emitted an astonishing quantity. The first was at that time nearly driėd up, and this induced the workmen to believe that the whole would one day cease, which perhaps has been the case. The tar was about the consistence of treacle, and beautifully pellucid. I have no doubt but it is the dregs of this very tar which at the distance of seven miles they extract from the coal. . . . It was from this place (Bridgnorth) where I remember in my former tour, I complained of eating musty chickens and tainted ham, that I went to see Coalbrookdale. I found the country beautifully picturesque, and if I could have satisfied my hunger by the food I took in at my eyes I should have had no reason to complain.

It was our intention, I remember, to stay all the night, but this was impossible, for the day was insufferably hot, and the prodigious piles of coal burning to coke, the furnaces, the forges, and the other tremendous objects emitting fire and smoke to an immense extent, together with the intolerable stench of the sulphur, approached very nearly to an idea of being placed in an air pump. We were glad enough to get away and sleep at Shifnal.

Affected as we were with the thick atmosphere, if it may be called so, in this strange region, we nevertheless noted some of its most remarkable objects, and among them of course the Iron Bridge which was then a great curiosity to me, as I had at that time never seen that at Bridgwater, or the other at Sunderland. I think this is the most beautiful of the three; for though it seems like network wrought in iron, it will apparently lay uninjured for ages. Coalbrookdale wants nothing but Cerberus to give you an idea of the heathen hell. The Severn may pass for the Styx, with this difference that Charon, turned turnpike man, ushers you over the bridge instead of rowing in his crazy boat; the men and women might easily be mistaken for devils and fairies, and the entrance of any one of these blazing caverns where they polish the cylinders, for Tartarus; and, really, if an atheist who had never heard of Coalbrookdale, could be transported there in a dream, and left to awake at the mouth of one of those furnaces, surrounded on all sides by such a number of infernal objects, though he had been all his life the most profligate unbeliever that ever added blasphemy to incredulity, he would infallibly tremble at the last judgement that in imagination would appear to him.

XX

The most thorough and most reliable account of the industries of the Coalbrookdale coalfield at the height of their prosperity is that which appears in Archdeacon Plymley's account of Shropshire agriculture published in 1803. The chapters on canals and industries were written by Thomas Telford, and information was collected from such eminent iron-masters and landowners as Edward Harries of Benthall, and William Reynolds. The list of ironworks makes an interesting contrast with Robert Townson's compiled about seven years earlier, on which it is obviously based. The account of the alkali works at Wombridge is one of the few records of the concern. The author of the account of the works, a Dr. Dugard of the Royal Salopian Infirmary, had previously practised near Coalbrookdale, and was recommended to the post at the Infirmary by William Reynolds, whose interests in chemistry, botany and mineralogy he shared.

Source: Joseph Plymley, *A General View of the Agriculture of Shropshire*, pp. 72, 82-3, 296-7, 315, 340-1.

The River Severn runs through this county, from North West to South East, and is navigable the whole way; but its navigation is very much impeded by the lowness of the water in summer and by floods in winter. It is the only navigable river. The vessels chiefly used on it are barges, trows, wherries and boats. The barges and trows have masts, which can be lowered to go under bridges: the stream carried them down, with or without a sail, and they are towed up by men, assisted or not, in the same manner, according to the wind. The barges are from 20 to 80 tons burthen, and trade very much between Shrewsbury and Gloucester. The trows are larger and belong to the ports lower down the Severn. They fetch timber from Pool-quay in Montgomeryshire; and are used to convey goods between Gloucester and Bristol, that are carried in smaller vessels to or from the first of these ports; but much the greater number of barges is employed in carrying the produce of the mines near Coalbrook-dale into the counties of Worcester, Gloucester, &c. A horse towing path is now established from Bewdley to Coalbrook-dale, which is more and more used, and, it is hoped, will soon be extended; the office of towing barges by men, being looked upon as very injurious to their manners. Coracles are another kind of vessel used upon this river by fisher-men, who are skilful in the management of them whilst upon the water,

67

and who carry them home, by depending them from the top of their heads, down their backs . . . Wine and grocery goods are brought up the Severn, from Bristol and Gloucester, to Shrewsbury, and so on to Montgomeryshire, and from Coalbrook-dale many vessels are laden with coal, and with the produce of their iron-works, potteries, china &c. The opposite shore of Broseley affords also the same ladings. There is limestone on both sides the river, but it is no great export, except when burnt into lime. There is a wharf, or quay, for vessels at Bridgnorth some miles below Coalbrook-dale and the same convenience at Shrewsbury, considerably higher up the river; but there is no great port in this county; perhaps 50,000 tons of coal are exported annually from Coalport, and a considerable quantity of goods, for the supply of Wellington, Newport, Shifnal, &c. are imported there. The principal warehouse extends over the canal, and is upon the bank of the Severn, so that goods can be taken up through a trap-door out of the canal, and let down into the vessels in the river, or vice-versa. Flannels are exported from Shrewsbury, and grain, cheese and lead. Soap is both imported to Shrewsbury from Bristol, by retail dealers, and soap made in Shrewsbury is exported down the river, and starch . . .

(The Shropshire Canal) . . . This canal, carried over high and rugged ground, along banks of slipping loam, over old coal mines and over where coal mines and iron stone are now actually worked under it, is a satisfactory proof that there is scarcely any ground so difficult, but where, with proper exertions and care, a convenient water conveyance may always be arranged . . .

On the banks of the Severn, Coalport, also established by the genius and laudatory exertions of Mr. William Reynolds, bids fair to rival Stourport, and becomes a station for such articles as are brought up the Severn, not only for the consumption of the adjoining country, but for most of the eastern parts of the county of Salop and also for a portion of Staffordshire . . .

Since the year 1797 the works at Coalport which . . . were established by Mr. William Reynolds on the banks of the Severn at the termination of the Shropshire Canal, about two miles below the iron bridge, have succeeded to a very considerable degree, and they are striking proof of the good effects of an improved inland navigation. Formerly the place consisted of a very rugged uncultivated bank, which scarcely produced even grass, but owing to the judicious regulations and encouragement by Mr. Reynolds, joined to the benefit arising from the canal and river, houses to the number of 30 have been built here, and more are still wanted, to accommodate the people employed at a large china manufactory, a considerable earthenware manufactory, another for making ropes, one for bag making and one for chains, which are now taking the place of ropes for the use of mines and for other purposes.

In the china manufactory, not established more than five years, and in which perhaps the best, and including its dependencies, the most china is manufactured of any work of that sort in Great Britain, there are employed about

32. '. . . *the genius and laudatory exertions of Mr. William Reynolds. . . .*' (Joseph Plymley & Thomas Telford, 1802)

Portrait of William Reynolds (Wilson of Birmingham)

Ironbridge Gorge Museum Trust Ltd.

250 persons, and in the other works at this place, about 150 more, making in the whole 400 persons. (Thomas Telford, November 1800.)

'The number of blast furnaces for iron between Ketley and Willey, about seven miles distance, exceed any within the same space in the kingdom. We have no reason to apprehend that the coal will fail us. Some of our veins of coal and iron stone are said to make iron of the first quality. The consumption occasioned by the number of hands employed in these works has been a great spur to our agriculture.' (Edward Harries, Esq.)

'In the coal district are the following ironworks. In the South is Willey, Broseley, Calcutts and Barnetts Leasow: these are on the South side of the Severn. On the North side of the river is Madeley Wood, Coalbrookdale, Lightmoor, Horsehay, Old Park, Snedshill, Ketley, Donnington Wood, Queenswood and Wrockwardine Wood'.

33. '. . . *much the greatest number of barges is employed in carrying the produce of the mines near Coalbrookdale into the counties of Worcester, Gloucester, &c. . . .'* (Joseph Plymley, 1802)

A view of Lincoln Hill with the Ironbridge in the distance taken from the side of the River Severn (James Fittler, 1788)

'There are now (1802) on the south side of the river Severn, at the different coal and iron works, 25 fire engines, and on the north side of the river 155, making altogether 180 engines. Thirty years ago I believe there were not 20 in the same district. The second lever engine that was erected was upon a colliery in Madeley Parish.' (Mr. W. Reynolds.)

Garden pots and other vessels of a coarse fabric are made at Broseley. At Caughley, in that neighbourhood, is a china manufacture of great excellence. The blue and white, and blue, white and gold china there, is, in many instances, more like that from the East than any other I have seen. These works have been purchased by the proprietors of a later establishment, the Coalport China works, and are confined to the ware specified above. At Coalport coloured china of all sorts, and of exquisite taste and beauty, is made. More immediately at Coalport, for the china works are near it, is a manufacture of earthenware, in imitation of that made at Etruria, and called the Queen's or Wedgwood ware . . .

. . . At Kingley Wich, about two miles west of Lilleshall-hill is a 'spring of salt water', that yields 4 to 5,000 gallons in the 24 hours. It is an impure brine, but was formerly used; the salt pans and buildings are still remaining.

It flows out of a reddish sandstone-rock which rests upon a reddish chert, like that of the Wrekin . . . The brine is now used for the making of soda, at a work established at Wormbridge, on the banks of the canal there, as will be seen by the following note, which is one of the many favours I have received from Mr. Dugard of the Salop Informaty:

'At Wormbridge, near Wellington, as well as at several other collieries in the neighbourhood, martial pyrites are found in considerable quantities. After being cleared from the coal (sulphureous coal) in which they are found, the lumps, which are perhaps from twelve to fourteen pounds weight each, are disposed in loose heaps, upon a bed, or large area, paved with bricks, and inclining from the circumference to the centre, to allow the water with which the whole is repeatedly sprinkled, ultimately to flow into a large reservoir which is constructed at this place. The pyrites are thus exposed to the action of the air as well as frequent waterings; the decomposition of them, produced by this process, forms sulphate of iron (martial vitriol) in considerable quantities, and was a few years ago evaporated and crystallized, and allowed to be by the consumers, as pure a salt of iron as any ever made in Great Britain. The demand for it was greater than the work, in its infant state, could supply. It is now no longer carried on as a vitriol manufactory; but the acid obtained from the pyrites, is wholly consumed in getting the soda from rock-salt and the brine of Kingley-wich'.

XXI

Of all foreign visitors to English ironworks in the 18th century, Swedes were perhaps the most numerous. There are several accounts of visits to the Coalbrookdale area by Swedes, one as early as 1753. Erik T. Svedenstierna, author of the journal from which these extracts are taken was in England in 1802-03, during the short period of peace which followed the Treaty of Amiens. His description of his travels was published in Stockholm in 1804, a German version appeared in 1811, and this translation in 1969.

The Swedish miles mentioned in the journal were equivalent to 7 kilometres, or 4.35 miles. The account is particularly valuable for its detailed description of the tar and coke works of Lord Dundonald, which adjoined the Calcutts ironworks 'Orsay', of course, means Horsehay. The ironworks belonging to Mr. Reynolds, was the Madeley Wood, or Bedlam works. Svedenstierna's account of iron bridges is a little confusing. The one at 'Little Wenlock' was probably Telford's bridge at Buildwas, and the third in the district that at Preens Eddy (now Coalport) which was partly of wood and partly of iron, and was replaced by the present Coalport bridge about 1818.

Source: W. A. Smith, 'A Swedish View of the West Midlands in 1802-03', The Polytechnic, Wolverhampton, *Journal of West Midland Studies III* (1970), pp. 45-54. (A full version of the journal with an introduction by Professor M. W. Flinn was published in 1973 under the title 'Svedenstierna's Tour in Great Britain, 1802-03; The Travel Diary of an Industrial Spy'.)

Broseley is a small town in Shropshire and lies on a hill on the south bank of the Severn. It is surrounded by coalmines and ironstone workings, some of which are even worked in the town and beneath it. On the slope of this hill close to the river, there are several ironworks and foundries, lime and brick kilns, tar ovens, and various other works and manufactories which form an uninterrupted chain of houses and buildings from Broseley right up to the renowned iron bridge near to Coalbrookdale, and extend for a distance of almost a quarter of a Swedish mile. On the opposite bank there is a similar concentration of furnaces, iron foundries, etc., above which, on the slope of the hill, one can see horse-gins, steam engines, and the air conduits or ventilators of the coalmines there. On the same side, below the iron bridge, houses extend for some considerable distance, in fact as far as Coalbrookdale, so called, which is somewhat more than a

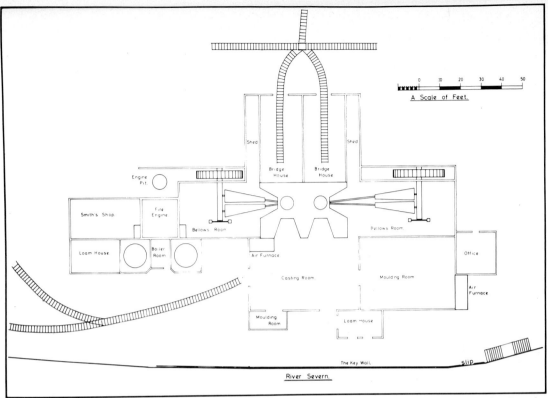

34. *'Straight opposite Broseley, below the iron bridge, there were two blast furnaces and a foundry which belong to a Mr. Reynolds. . . .'* (Erik T. Svedenstierna, 1802)

Plan of Madeley Wood furnaces, 1772

Re-drawn by the late Derek Jobber from British Museum Map Kxxxvi.16.1

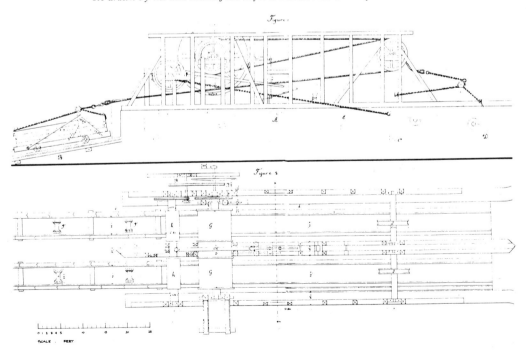

35. *'Further down . . . was an inclined plane, on which loaded boats were drawn up and down between the river and the canal situated higher up. . . .'* (Erik T. Svedenstierna, 1802)

Jean Dutens' drawings of The Hay inclined plan, Coalport

From 'Etudes sur les Travaux Publiques d'Angleterre', 1819

quarter of a Swedish mile from Broseley. Here there are several lime-stone mines in the hills on both sides of the Severn, from which the stone is brought down to the lime-kilns situated on the banks, either on an inclined plane or through mine galleries. Although a traveller must think the mass of houses, building and works on this area to be a single town, it is divided up here into Broseley, Ironbridge and Coalbrookdale. The latter name in fact relates to the valley itself which comes to an end to the north of the iron bridge and in which there are several ironworks named Dale Works or Dale Company Works.

Close to Broseley, in the lower region of the aforementioned plain near the Severn, is the Calcutts ironworks belonging to Mr. Brodie of London. It consists of three furnaces, some foundries or so-called Air-furnaces, a cannon boring machine and a turning shop together with more work places belonging to foundries. The furnaces, of which two were then in blast, and one undergoing repair, are not as tall as those in South Wales, and like the rest of the furnaces hereabouts rarely produce more than 30 tons of iron per week since the two above mentioned furnaces together produce around 50 tons per week. The pig iron here is altogether better and more suitable for fine and strong castings. The boring of cannon is done here with the aid of a steam-engine which works directly on a crank fastened in the centre of a shaft and this crank subsequently operated 11 horizontal borers via connecting rods.

At this works approximately 20 ovens have been built in order to collect, after the manner of Lord Dundonald's invention, the bitumen of pit-coal in the process of reducing the coal to coke. The ovens are arch-shaped and built with bricks, and have, inside and outside, the appearance of a hay-rick or beehive 7 to 8 ft. in height and diameter. On the side of the oven is an opening, through which the pit-coal is introduced, and on the floor is a square hole with strong and closely-spaced grate bars, under which there is a space for ashes and which is connected with an opening in the outer wall. In the oven dome itself there is another opening into which is fitted a cast-iron pipe several inches in diameter, which then enters a brick built water reservoir. When the oven has been filled it is heated through the ash-hole, and as soon as the coal is burning sufficiently the large opening is walled up. The smoke then passes through the pipe in the roof and is condensed in the water reservoir. A quantity of hydrogen gas or combustible air develops during condensation and is led away from the reservoir through another pipe. The tar is drawn off from the reservoir into a large tank where it is left in order that the impurities be deposited and most of the water be separated. The tar is at this stage still unsuitable for most uses and must therefore undergo a kind of distillation and as a result of this distillation and being mixed with a little water changes to a strong viscous oil, which is similar to our pitch oil. The oil is used to paint certain parts of buildings, and mixed with lamp-black to touch up fences and suchlike.

The remaining refined tar is used either like other tar or boiled down to pitch. Here they seemed to be content with this equipment, although they also maintained that this tar, admittedly useful for some purposes, damaged ropework and that on the whole the invention was of little value.

The so-called valley works (Dale works) begin on the outskirts of Coalbrookdale and extend up the valley to an ironworks called Orsay, which also belongs to the Dale Company. The latter works has a better appearance and seems to have built later than the others. It consists of two blast furnaces and some refineries, puddling furnaces and rolling mills. In the works situated further down the valley there are merely two blast furnaces, and some foundries, together with grinding and turning machines. A considerable quantity of small castings such as fire-grates, weights, flat-irons, stoves and screws for cider presses is produced here, and these products are mostly cast from reverberatory furnaces or from so called cupolas in which iron fragments and all kinds of small broken iron are smelted with an ordinary blower. These cupolas are square, no more than a few feet high and the outside is clad with pig-iron plates and the inside with refractory bricks. The hearth is very small and often not more than an inch in diameter.

All furnaces and rolling mills at the Daleworks are driven by the customary large steam-engines, but the turning and grinding machines are operated by water of a small brook which winds down the valley. Further down the valley from the latter works and not far from the iron bridge there was a machine for boring cylindrical bellows, and a forge hammer constructed just as in our country, both of which were driven by water. The frame of the hammer was mostly of wood but the hammer head, the waterwheel and the hammer shaft were of pig-iron.

When the forgeman was instructed to show me the process of flattening with the aid of such a hammer, as these are very rare in England, he raised the guard too soon as that the hammer hit the anvil itself 7 or 8 times before the piece of iron was in place. I could only imagine that the hammer and anvil would be ruined as a result but the smith assured me that this was a common occurrence and that the equipment was never damaged. I am mentioning this here in order to illustrate how these people have mastered the art of giving cast iron any required characteristic.

Straight opposite Broseley, below the iron bridge, there were two blast furnaces and a foundry which belong to a Mr. Reynolds. A blowing cylinder 7 feet in diameter provides the blast for both furnaces, and has a regulator, consisting of a cylinder upside down in water, which the air enters near the base before going into the blast furnace through the opening opposite. The water, the level of which was fixed and constant before the blower started working, served as a counterweight, and had the same function as the moveable cover on an upright cylinder, as is the usual way of regulating the blast in England.

Further down, on the same side of the Severn, was an inclined plane, on which loaded boats were drawn up and down between the river and the canal situated higher up.

In the neighbourhood there was also a porcelain factory, which, however, I could not inspect. Nevertheless I saw tea-cups made here which come very near in whiteness to the best Paris porcelain, and which had a more beautiful gilding than I had seen before in England. The English are only just really starting to compete with the best porcelain factories.

At a coalmine above Mr. Reynold's furnace was a small steam-engine of 3 horse power which drew coal from a depth of several fathoms. The boiler of this small machine was built into the chimney, which served as a ventilator of the mine so that a separate firing for the last mentioned purpose was obviated.

Several features of this area immediately attract the attention of the traveller and the iron bridge is one of these. I cannot in fact recall the length of the arch but this has frequently been recorded; however, I must mention an incident which testifies to the strength of such bridges. Shortly before I visited the area, the bridge which continued to be used regardless, was affected by subsidence of the ground at one end, to such an extent that a number of bolts either broke or bent, and it was clearly seen that certain parts of the structure had begun to separate. These parts were screwed together, the arch was tightened as much as possible, and the displaced abutment meanwhile strengthened, without the bridge having once been taken out of use on this account.

Otherwise this bridge is less remarkable with regard to its appearance and size since several bridges have been built in England which are larger and more imposing however, it was the first of its kind and served to demonstrate the value of such bridges. Besides the old iron bridge at Coalbrookdale two others were recently built over the Severn, one north of Broseley, and one south of the Ironbridge in the middle of the village of Little Wenlock. The latter has a much lighter and prettier appearance than the old bridge. In all the ironworks, as at the mines, there are many large and small railways, which are sometimes 1 to 2 miles long.

The coal seams here are very near to the surface, they are more irregular and have more falls than in South Wales, and are usually of greater thickness. Haulage takes place by means of horse-gins or small steam-engines and the shafts are rarely more than 8 to 10 fathoms deep and sometimes not more than 5 fathoms.

The method of working is quite simple: the coal is removed from a limited area around the base of the shaft and also as much ironstone as is needed and then the mine is abandoned. Everywhere in this district one frequently comes across caved-in shafts and hollows in the earth in areas where there are houses and gardens. Some houses had recently collapsed and others were standing at such an angle that I don't understand how people could live in them.

Less than a Swedish half mile from Ironbridge, on the left hand side of the road to Shifnal, is the Lightmoor Ironworks, whose manager is a Mr. Homfray, the brother of Mr. Homfray of Pendarran.

It consists of three blast furnaces, and a few refineries and bloom or balling furnaces. Most cast iron is here run into pigs from which fine metal and iron stock is made, which is sent into Worcestershire to be worked up into plate bar-iron, nail rods, etc., in different works belonging to the Lightmoor Company.

All around Lightmoor were railways, belonging partly to the nearby mines and partly to the Shropshire Canal, where small wagons containing limestone were drawn down a steep slope to the loading place. This limestone came a distance of a few miles in square-ended boats capable of carrying 8 tons of cargo, but which on account of the lack of water could only be laden with 5 tons. Several boats were attached one behind the other and in this manner a horse could pull 100 tons or more.

At a mine, where the haulage was carried out by means of a steam-engine with a rope wound over a horizontal roller, a sort of flat rope was used, about 3 inches wide and a finger thick. These ropes are as if plaited, and in this respect are not unlike braided watchcords. These ropes had been tried out for too short a time for any assessment to be made of their advantages over other ropes with respect to their durability, but otherwise they performed like usual ropes.

XXII

After the death of John Fletcher of Madeley in 1785, his work was continued by his wife Mary whom he had married four years earlier. Mary Fletcher was allowed to choose the curates who served the parish church, she worked closely with the Wesleyan ministers stationed in Shropshire, and Madeley was the focus of all Evangelical activities in the district. This account of what happened at Madeley on a typical Sunday around 1800 was written by William Tranter, a native of Coalbrookdale, and a convert of Mary Fletcher. He became a Wesleyan minister and lived to be a centenarian. The room mentioned in the second sentence was the Vicarage Barn, which was demolished about 1830.

Source: *Methodist Magazine,* 1837, pp. 901-02.

On the Sabbath, the pious people, living at the distance of from one to three or four miles from Madeley, usually arrived in time for Mrs. Fletcher's morning meeting. In fine weather the room used generally to be full. The religious services for the day were as follows:—after Prayer, with which the service always commenced, a beautifully prepared piece called the 'Watchword', occupying from ten minutes to a quarter of an hour, was read . . . At the close of this exercise, Mrs. Fletcher spoke to a few, chiefly aged persons, coming from a distance, on their religious experience, giving to each advice, encouragement or admonition. If any strangers were present, as was often the case, she now gave them an invitation to express, for the edification of others, their own views and feelings. And here she appeared to great advantage. The pious counsel and caution she would address to such strangers, displayed great insight into human nature, clear and comprehensive views of the method of salvation, intimate knowledge of the deep things of God, amazing unction of the Spirit, deep personal piety, and a rich experience of the power of religion. If time permitted, after these strangers, any persons present might speak on their own religious experience; and thus the happy moments flew away only too rapidly, but leaving solid and lasting benefits behind.

The chiming of the church going bell was then heard, and the assembly separated to meet again in the parish church close at hand, to which the people very generally repaired, Mrs. Fletcher always, if in health; and for its services the preceding exercised were found to be a happy and profitable preparation. Here too the Gospel, in those days, gave no uncertain sound.

36. *'The chiming of the church going bell was then heard, and the assembly separated to meet
again in the parish church close at hand. . . .'* (William Tranter)

Madeley Church, Vicarage and Vicarage Barn (S. Lacey)

Salop County Record Office

Here the sacred truths of vital and spiritual Christianity were faithfully and
affectionately announced from the pulpit, as, during the week, they were
illustrated in the life of the preacher.

The noon hour of the Sabbath was generally spent in the following manner:—
respectable strangers visiting Madeley for religious purposes, when discovered
as such, were usually invited to dine with Mrs. Fletcher at the vicarage-house,
where they were sure to find a cheerful welcome to things necessary for the
refreshment, and at the same time, by edifying conversation, a feast for the
soul. The poor, living too far off to allow them to return from their own
houses for the after services of the day, partook, if so disposed, of her
hospitalities in the vicarage kitchen. Some, having brought their provisions
with them, were seen in fine weather in little companies in the fields,
holding heavenly conversation and prayers. Others of the respectable portion
of these pious persons, wishing to enjoy the remainder of the Sabbath
services, had, in an apartment to themselves, a cheap family dinner provided

37. '... *And here she appeared to great advantage....*' (William Tranter)
Portrait of Mary Fletcher (Anon)
From H. Moore, 'Life of Mrs. Fletcher', 1817

at the village inn, where great decorum was maintained. Here they, too, spent the time in edifying conversation and prayer, till the welcome little bell reminded them of Mrs. Fletcher's one o'clock meeting. At these meetings, for the most part numerously attended, she read the Life of some eminently holy person, such as Wesley, Whitefield, Walsh &c. This was accompanied with such remarks of her own on the excellency or defects of the character under consideration as showed her great spiritual discernment, and rendered the memoir, thus read, additionally instructive.

On the ringing of the bell for the afternoon service, this exercise was suspended. At church there was always a sermon in the afternoon; and those who could make it convenient remained to hear it, and to join in the other devotions of the Church. Those who could not, by reason of distance or other circumstances, remain, now repaired to their homes, to be in readiness for the evening services in their own vicinity, there being several large chapels in the populous parts of the parish, at each of which the Minister officiated every Sabbath evening alternately, as well as occasionally on the week days, always announcing at the close of the afternoon service in the church at which chapel he should preach that evening. This plan was adopted by Mr. Fletcher, and was followed by his evangelical and pious successors for upwards of forty years.

William Tranter.

XXIII

The Shropshire iron trade entered a period of crisis after the ending of the wars with France in 1815. By comparison with works in other parts of Britain those in Shropshire were largely obsolete. Thomas Butler, of the Kirkstall Force near Leeds, made a tour of Midlands Ironworks in the summer of 1815, in company with a Mr. Buckley, a Manchester iron merchant. His journal shows clearly the depression into which the Shropshire iron industry had fallen by this time. The canal inclined plane he visited on 1st September was that at Windmill Farm.

Source: Alan Birch, 'The Midlands Iron Industry during the Napoleonic Wars', *Edgar Allen News*, Aug./Sept. 1952.

1st September, Friday.

Over the Iron Bridge, on the left, 2 furnaces on the banks of the Severn belonging Mr. Phillips & Cox, called Barnett Leasow. The iron is marked BLF—this iron is always esteemed of superior quality, nearly equal to Madeley Wood, only one furnace in blast, about 20 tons stock; they are not averaging more than 25 tons per week.

A little further down the river are two furnaces out of blast, both repairing, pigs are marked Callcott, belonging late Alex. Brodie of London . . . there made a middling sort of iron, but appears almost in ruins. About one mile up the hill on the right is Broseley furnace—Onions & Co. This is an old work almost in ruins.

Returned back to the Severn river, was taken over in a boat which was ferried by old Charon in a very curious manner.

On our road to Shifnal we stopped the chaise at the canal bridge near Madeley where we observed the Inclined Plane, 900 ft. long, which rises (we could not get the elevation) up and down by means of a steam engine. Vessels laden with iron, coal etc. are drawn with amazing facility from the lower to the higher level of the canal—this prevents any waste of water— each vessel contains about five tons of coal or iron and may be drawn up in about five minutes; or as the boy and man said, about 8 times an hour. . . . We rode down the plane upon one of the carriages on which was fixed a boat laden with coals.

2nd September, Saturday.

Went to the three Madeley Wood furnaces very near the Iron Bridge. Two in blast, belonging to Reynolds and Anstice. These have been perhaps the most

38. *'Returned back to the Severn river, was taken over in a boat which was ferried by an old Charon in a very curious manner'* (Thomas Butler, 1815)

A ferry in the Severn Gorge, *c.* 1910

Photo: Ironbridge Gorge Museum

39. *'Went to the three Madeley Wood furnaces very near the Iron Bridge'* (Thomas Butler, 1815)

The Madeley Wood furnaces under restoration, 1973

Photo: The Author

40. *'We rode down the plane upon one of the carriages on which was fixed a boat laden with coals'* (Thomas Butler, 1815)

The Hay Inclined Plane, Coalport, in the late 19th century

Photo: Ironbridge Gorge Museum

profitable iron concerns in the country . . . the manager of the Madeley Wood furnaces is Williams brother to William Williams, formerly a puddler at Kirkstall Forge, who was brought thither by Robert Adams. Williams says that before he took the management of the works they consumed more than 6 tons of coals to a ton of pig iron, and Mr. Phillips of Barnett Leasow works, whom we met at Shrewsbury, says they even now consume 7 tons in making best iron.

Notwithstanding the high price that the Madeley Wood iron fetches, I understand the company considers the coal trade far more lucrative than the iron trade . . . I have observed generally that the wages in Staffordshire are at least 15% higher than in Shropshire, if the information I have been able to collect be correct. They seldom exceed 25 tons No. 1 good iron per week, but they can make 35 tons good grey strong forge. It is always admitted that the Madeley Wood pig iron is some of the best in England.

83

I could not learn any other reason given why this is the case only that the crow or cross stone was a peculiar kind of ironstone and a small quantity of it used along with other mines gave the iron that peculiarly soft quality.

41. *'About one mile up the hill on the right is Broseley furnace. . . . This is an old work almost in ruins. . . .'* (Thomas Butler, 1815)

Old Furnaces, Broseley (J. Homes Smith, 1821)
Shropshire Archaeological Society, Homes Smith Collection, Salop County Library

Coalbrookdale. Two furnaces, Darby & Co. both in blast. These furnaces are blown by a water wheel, all the machinery old and clumsy and all the works seem to be conducted upon the old plans of forty years ago. Did not examine the lower mills but there the machinery is the same, I understand. They are making at one furnace only 20 tons per week. The upper furnace about 28 tons—the iron pretty good. They use all themselves in castings and into wrought iron.

Great fortunes have been made here—no wonder, they had formerly no opposition, but had everything their own way. I imagine that now they are doing little good but being very opulent they can afford to do little business. Consequently they are doing little harm and I imagine never more will they do much good, for the minerals now lay at a considerable distance; and to make these works do equally to the Staffordshire and Welsh people they must be entirely new built from the very foundations.

84

Horsehay. Three furnaces—one in blast, there are slitting and rolling mills and all together is a very considerable works, belonging to Darby & Co. also, but not one half employed; I suppose for the same reasons as at the Dale. They can do no good just now, therefore, they will do no harm.

. . . There appeared so little doing at these works that we tarried very little. They gave us a melancholy picture of the iron trade. The proprietors being very rich, as was mentioned before, they afford to do little.

. . . Thence to Ketley works, William Reynolds & Co., this is an old established work and has been for a very long time conducted in the most respectable manner; large fortunes have been made here. The counting houses are very spacious, divided into different offices for the various departments, occupied by several clerks, and a noble office for the principals. The whole may be compared to the Commons, Lords and Kings.

XXIV

John Thornton, a Northamptonshire landowner, kept a diary of visits he made while staying in Shropshire in the summer of 1819, which includes an interesting description of a railway inclined plane. He was one of a relatively small number of visitors to the area who inspected the works of the Botfield family. He met Thomas Botfield at Stirchley, although the concern he visited was probably the ironworks at Old Park, Dawley, not far away.

Source: MS. Journal of a Journey undertaken by John Thornton, describing visits to country houses and industrial sites, Aug.–Sept. 1819, Northants. Record Office. Th. 3182.

On Monday the 23rd August we rode through Cottesbrook & Sutton to Colebrook Dale with which were much delighted. We passed through Coal Port, where there is a Wooden Bridge, & road through the Valley to the Iron Bridge near which there is an Inn where we put up our Horses and ate some hot roast beef tarts after which we walked about the Place. Colebrook Dale is valley through which the Severn runs, having steep ascent on each side, on which there is a large Village, chiefly consisting in Iron manufactories, & storehouses. There are a great number of steam engines & furnaces as well as Iron Railways on which small waggons loaded with Ironstone or Coal run down an inclined plane from the Pitts which are at the top of the Hill. The waggons are not drawn by horses but are constructed in such a manner that by the assistance of chains & windlasses, the weight of the loaded waggons running down the inclined Plane draws the empty waggon up again to the top of the hill.

Women are employed to separate the Iron stone from the common soil, which by practice they perform with great expedition. We afterwards walked to the furnaces, where the iron is separated from the dross, & formed into short bars, called Pigs, in which form it is sent to London, Liverpool & other places. The Coal is obliged to be reduced almost to cinder, before it can be used, by which means the sulphur is extracted from it. The Dross is called Slag, & is used to mend the Roads with. In our return we passed over both the Iron and the wooden Bridges which are almost the extremities of the Dale.

On Wednesday we rode to Stirchley where we met Mr. T. Botfield, who conducted us round his Iron works. They were nearly similar to what we

42. *'We rode to Stirchley where we met Mr. T. Botfield, who conducted us round his Iron works. They were nearly similar to what we had seen at Colebrook Dale, but on rather a larger scale'* (John Thornton, 1819)

Near Wellington, Shropshire [probably the Stirchley Ironworks] (Francis Nicholson, 1821)

Ironbridge Gorge Museum Trust

had seen at Colebrook Dale, but on rather a larger scale. We saw at Stirchley a Steam Engine, the power of which was equal to 30 Horses, & a machine, like a pair of scissors, which would cut any Iron Bar through with the greatest ease. We had seen a machine of similar use to this at Portsmouth. The Iron railways which run in every direction about the Iron works cost 1000 Pounds a mile laying down and the fires by which the Steam boilers are heated consume nearly 1000 tons of Coals per day. Mr. Botfield used to live at Stirchley but has now removed to Decker Hill. We were entertained with a Luncheon by the Rector of the Place, after which we rode round Mr. Botfields farm & through Shiffnal to Decker Hill where we met the rest of our party who had come in the Carriage, & Mr. Smith. We had a magnificent Dinner & returned to Badger in the Evening.

XXV

Joshua Field (1787-1863) was an engineer who worked with Henry Maudslay on the development of marine engines in London, and was one of the founders of the Institute of Civil Engineers. He made a tour of the Midlands in 1821. His account of the Severn Gorge largely confirms the gloomy picture of the iron industry painted by Thomas Butler. He saw two interesting events actually taking place: the demolition of the great 'Resolution' steam engine at Coalbrookdale, which had pumped water from the lower to the upper pools of the ironworks, and the replacement of the wooden land arches of the Iron Bridge, erected about 1800, by iron arches. The Iron Bridge was erected in 1779-81, and not in 1784, and the Lightmoor ironworks did not, as Field suggests, belong to the Coalbrookdale partners in 1821.

Source: J. W. Hall, 'Joshua Field's Diary of a Tour in 1821 through the Midlands', in *Transactions of the Newcomen Society,* Vol. VI (1925-26), pp. 30-32.

. . . in the evening went in a Chaise to Colnbrookdale, at which place we arrived at ½ past 10 at night. When we descended the hill the numerous furnaces below seemed to fill the whole valley with fire and produced an effect dreadful and grand.

Sunday, August 26, 1821.

Walked through the dale works which are in a great measure deserted, the lease being nearly out, the company are at little pains to keep them up. The Blast furnaces are not worked and nothing is doing here but some castings, and a little bad mill work. A Wretched bad sugar mill is making from drawings sent from the west indies from which they cannot alter anything. The foreman does not know how the thing is to perform, it is with three horizontal rollers; a small forge or 2 is working from the stream of water which originally led to ironworks being established here but the great engine which supplied the deficiency of this stream is now taken partly down and the Furnaces are all removed to where the iron stone coal etc. are found and the furnaces blown by steam. We walked on to Horshays one of the Companys works. Here are three Blast Furnaces, 2 at work and a large rolling mill of 60 HP tolerably good but old and dirty.

The furnaces are situated by the side of a hill so that the filling houses are level with the tops of the furnaces; this is a general way in Shropshire

43. *'The iron bridge at Coalbrookdale seems to stand very well . . . 2 side arches of wood . . . are now so decayed that iron arches are putting up in their place. . . .'*
(Joshua Field, 1821)
Iron Bridge, Coalbrook Dale (W. Smith, 1810)
Ironbridge Gorge Museum Trust

tho' not in Staffordshire. A foundry is attached to one of the blast furnaces in which furnace they always make better iron than in the other for some of it goes in castings—walked in the afternoon along the banks of the Severn through Madeley to Coalport as far as the inclined plane where boats are taken up from a small canal a few feet above the Severn into the Shropshire Canal about 100 ft. high. The machinery is very rude, the Whimsey a bad one, the railway strong but very much out of line, the rope barrels &c. well contrived.

Along the banks of the Severn are several iron furnaces: the Bedlam with 2 furnaces, the Calcot, belonging to Mr. Hazeldine & others, the mine coal and lime-stone all being very convenient. We crossed the Severn which is here about the width of the river at Richmond but very shallow and rapid. The ferry boats are decked a foot below the gunwhale. They have an anchor up the stream and a chain made of long links about ¼ diam. fixed from the anchor to the top of a short mast, then by the rudder and the man can steer the boat across the river without any trouble. We came to the tar works established by Lord Dundonald for extracting tar from coal and saving the coak.

89

44. '. . . the great engine which supplied the deficiency of this stream is now taken partly down. . . .'
(Joshua Field, 1821)
The Resolution Steam Engine, Coalbrookdale (W. Homes Smith, 1821)
Homes Smith Collection, Shropshire Archaeological Society, Salop County Library Local Studies Section

The iron bridge at Coalbrookdale seems to stand very well, it was built 1784. The great arch only was made of iron and 2 side arches of wood which are now so decayed that iron arches are putting up in their places. The ribs of the one ½ the bridge are up, and the road contracted to ½ the width. At Madeley I saw the most miserable engine driving a clay mill, both as to contrivance and execution.

Mon. August 27th.

We went to the Lightmoor works belonging to the Company about 3 miles from the Iron bridge; this is a large works for making pig iron, esteemed a good sort of Shropshire pig. They have three furnaces 2 in & 1 repairing into which we went.

XXVI

One of the best descriptions of Coalport almost at the height of its prosperity occurs in a directory published in Wem in 1824. It mentions almost every economic activity of the flourishing canal and riverside settlement.

Source: T. Gregory, *The Shropshire Gazetteer,* 1824, pp. 285-86

Two miles from (Madeley) church, in a south easterly direction, is Coalport, which takes its name from the termination of the Shropshire Canal, which is seven miles in length. The coals brought by this conveyance, from the extensive mines of Ketley, Dawley and other places, are landed on the banks of the river Severn, and are thence transported in barges to different parts of the counties of Worcester and Gloucester, to the average amount of fifty thousand tons annually.

The large and flourishing Porcelain Manufactory of John Rose and Co., the only one of the kind in this county, where the arts of modelling and painting have reached a high degree of perfection, is carried on at Coalport. This article, in the beauty of its composition—the superior taste displayed on its surface, and the elegance of the workmanship, is nowhere excelled. From four to five hundred persons are constantly employed in this manufacture, which is the sole support of at least fifteen hundred inhabitants of the Salopian soil, and the source from which many individuals have amassed great wealth. There is also a rope and timber yard, on an extensive scale, and a nearby iron bridge over the Severn, erected in 1817 in place of a wooden one.

Near this bridge is remarkably large wheel, 240 ft. in circumference. It turns a wheel for expressing oil from linseed. The mill is the property of William Horton, Esq., and not far from it, is the residence of that gentleman, delightfully situated on the banks of the river. About a mile distant, between the above mentioned bridge and the old one erected in 1779, are the large furnaces of the Madeley Wood Co., used for the making of pig iron of superior quality. At a little distance is a neat villa, the residence of William Anstice Esq., one of the proprietors of these works, and further to the left, is the Hay, a place of great antiquity, the seat of Robert Ferriday, Esq.

There is in this neighbourhood a tunnel made by order of the late William Reynolds, Esq., for the more easy conveyance of coals, which are here the

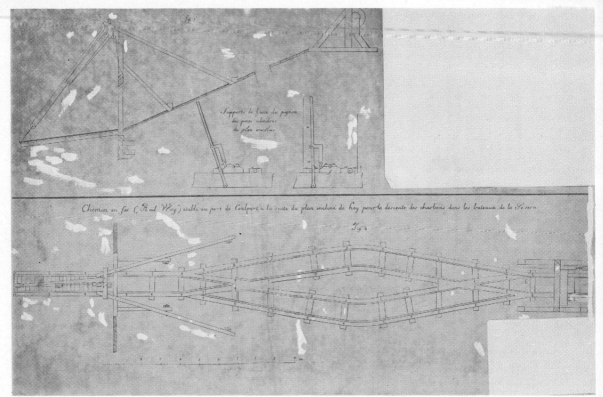

45. *'Coalport . . . takes its name from the termination of the Shropshire Canal. . . . The coals . . . are landed on the banks of the river Severn, and are thence transported in barges. . . .'* (T. Gregory, 1824)

Jean Dutens' drawings of the inclined railways used to carry coal between canal and river at Coalport

From 'Etudes sur les Travaux Publiques d'Angleterre', 1819

46. *'Near this bridge is a remarkably large wheel, 240 ft. in circumference'* (T. Gregory, 1824)

Wheel and Pot Works at Coalport, *c.* 1810

Ironbridge Gorge Museum Trust

chief article of commerce. This tunnel was discontinued from some unknown cause. Its length is about one mile in a direct line, and it is arched with brick nearly the whole way. It is remarkable that a quantity of the tar flows from the interstices in the sides. The tar, falling upon the surface of a small stream which flows in a channel to the entrance is there deposited in the form of a sediment, and at convenient times is put into barrels for use. The quantity thus obtained, when the excavation was first made, exceeded one barrel per day; and each barrel was worth about three guineas. But ever since that period the quantity has gradually diminished, and is now not more than twenty barrels in the year. It is therefore probable that in a few years, this bounty of nature will be exhausted.

XXVII

Karl August Ludwig Freiheer von Oeynhausen and Ernst Heinrich Karl von Dechen were two Prussian civil servants concerned with the mining industry who visited Britain in 1826–27 in order to gather information on railways. Oeyhausen (1795–1865) was born in Westphalia in 1795, studied at Gottingen, and in 1831 became Chief Mining Counsellor in Bonn for the Prussian government. As a result of his borings for salt at Neusalzwerk that town was named after him Bad Oeynhausen by King Frederick William IV in 1845. Dechen (1800–1889) was born in Berlin and joined the mining department of the Prussian government in 1820. He became Superintendent of Mines of the Rhine Provinces, based in Bonn in 1841, and played a prominent part in the civic life of that city. Oeynhausen and Dechen were the only visitors to notice the dual gauge plateway in Coalbrookdale, of which archaeological evidence came to light in 1970. They gave a very detailed description of the canal inclined plane at The Hay, and are the only visitors to describe it as single-tracked with a passing loop in the middle. This was certainly not the case when the incline was built, nor was it so by 1849, when a plan of it appears on the Madeley tithe map. Archaeological evidence may one day show whether they were right. It is possible that the confused the canal inclined plane with some of the railway inclines in the Ironbridge Gorge.

Source: C. von Oeynhausen and H. von Dechen, *Railways in England 1826 and 1827,* translated by E. A. Forward, ed. Charles E. Lee. *Newcomen Society,* 1971, pp. 67, 73–4.

In Coalbrookdale, a·cast iron tramroad runs from the Severn to the lower iron smelting works of the Dale Company. As is the case with all tramroads in this district it belongs to the same species (i.e. plateway). The rails are 5 and even 5½ feet long, and lie in cast iron sleepers. The tramroads at Coalbrookdale are of two sizes. The smaller one is of 20 in. gauge, and the haulage on this is performed with small trucks; it lies in the middle of a larger line of 36 in. gauge. Horse haulage is used thereon. It perhaps merits remark that the smallest gauge for horse use employed anywhere is to be found in this district, as on some lines the gauge is only 18 inches . . .

At the Horsehay Ironworks which also belongs to the Dale Company, there are tipping wagons with sheet iron bodies on wooden frames, very suitable for the transport of blast furnace slag. The wheels on these wagons are

47. *'The tramroads at Coalbrookdale are of two sizes. . . . The smaller one is of 20 in. gauge . . . it lies in the middle of a larger line of 36in. gauge. . . .'* (C. von Oeynhausen and H. von Dechen, 1826-7)

Dual gauge plateway uncovered at Rose Cottage, Coalbrookdale, 1971

Photo: Ironbridge Gorge Museum Trust

48. *'All these rails are so laid that the flange lies on the inner side, and at the same time holds together the hauling path. . . .'* (C. von Oeynhausen and H. von Dechen, 1826-7)

Coalbrookdale Company wrought iron plate rails, with a plateway tanker waggon, at the Blists Hill open air museum

Photo: The Author

from 14 to 18 in. diameter, and have wider wheel rims than are employed elsewhere in England, and especially in South Wales, namely 1¼ to 1½ in. All these rails are so laid that the flange lies on the inner side, and at the same time holds together the hauling path . . .

About 2 miles below Coalbrookdale, the Shropshire Canal is united with the Severn by a self-acting plane 793 ft. long and with a vertical drop of 207 ft. or an angle of 15½ degrees. The railway thereon is of cast iron built in the manner of a tramroad. The rails are the strongest and thickest of the kind that we have seen; also, they lie on longitudinal timbers 14 in. wide and thick, and these upon wooden cross sleepers. The whole inclined plane is well paved. The tramroad has three lines of rails, so that it forms two tracks with one common rail; in the middle of the plane, where the full and empty waggons pass one another, there are four lines of rails forming two separate tracks. On one track the rail flanges are inside and on the other track outside. The rails are 80 in. (6 ft. Engl.) long, 7 in. wide, exclusive of the 2½ in. high and 1 in. thick flange, and 2 in. thick. On one end there is a projecting point 5 in. broad and 1½ in. long and on the other end a suitable notch in which the point fits. In addition there is a tab on the flange through which a wooden plug is inserted to connect the two rails; four 1 in. square holes enable the rails to be spiked to the horizontal timbers.

The connection of the rails by wooden plugs is seldom used, and only a few rails are provided with the small recess in the middle of the flange. In the track are iron rollers over which the rope runs.

The canal boats which arrive on the Shropshire Canal are let down on this self-acting plane. A wooden wagon frame is used for lowering them. Most of the canal boats are of wood, 18 ft. long, 5 ft. 2 in. wide, and 2½ feet deep, in the clear. One such boat weighs about 1½ tons empty, and the greatest load amounts to about 5 tons, whereby it still has about 2 in. freeboard. The cargo consists of coal and iron.

The wooden frame on which the boats are placed is of very simple construction. On the two outer frame beams stand posts 5 ft. high, fixed by struts, and connected at the top by an iron cramp provided with three eyes for the attachment of the chain. The frame has two large front wheels 27 in. diameter, and two small hind wheels 16 in. diameter, which have an inside gauge of 43 in. They are 6 in. wide at the rim, and 10 in. long in the nave; these lie wholly under the frame. Outside of the wagon there are also two outer flanged wheels of 24 in. diameter, on the same axle as the small hind wheels, and with a gauge of 78 in. When the waggon is drawn out of the canal upon the bank of the self-acting plane, these wheels run upon a special railway, and thereby enable it to pass over the highest point of the bank without rubbing. The weight of the wagon frame is 2 tons, and the boat with its load 6½ tons, therefore the total weight is 8½ tons or 170 cwt. About 100 boats can be let down in 12 hours.

A 26 in. steam engine stands on the highest point of the self-acting plane, on the ridge formed by it and the short inclined plane leading to the canal. This serves to draw the waggon with the canal boat out of the upper part of the canal. It also completes the drawing up of the waggon coming up the self-acting plane, when the full wagon, with the boat, has plunged into the water, and thus so reduced its effective weight that it is no longer able to draw the empty wagon right to the top of the plane.

On the axle of the steam engine there is a small gear wheel with 24 teeth, which engages with a larger wheel with 96 teeth, on the axle of which is fitted the rope drum of 7 ft. diameter, with the brake wheels for the self-acting plane. The small gear wheel can be put in or out of gear by a contrivance operated in the engine house, so that the engine and the rope drum can move independently of one another. The rope goes from this drum over it on rope sheaves 6 ft. diameter, and 5 in wide, and then under the drum away to the self-acting plane; the rope sheaves hang perpendicularly over the upper part of the canal, so that the wagon can be drawn forward over the ridge. A pinion with 40 teeth on the axle of the steam engine engages with a wheel with 96 teeth mounted on an intermediate axle which also carries a pinion with 28 teeth. This intermediate axle has a bearing-seat inside the engine house, and can be put in or out of gear by means of a lever, so that this axle can be put in motion or at rest according to choice. The pinion of 28 teeth engages with a wheel of 80 teeth which is mounted on the axle of a small chain drum and brake wheel; through this drum, and a chain, the canal boat is drawn out of the upper part of the canal on to the top of the self-acting plane. The manipulation of the brake is as follows:—as soon as the full wagon comes to the bottom the laden boat is removed by a workman and pushed into the canal, and in exchange an empty boat is brought on and affixed. The full down-going boat does not draw up the empty one the whole distance, because the tramroad goes entirely under the surface in the lower canal, and the loaded boat, as soon as it plunges into the water, loses much of its weight. As soon as the empty boat stops, a workman releases the brake on the large rope drum, while another puts the engine in connection with this drum and sets it in motion so that the boat shall continue its journey upward and across the ridge of the self-acting plane. When the boat has reached the ridge it goes slowly on the tramroad into the upper canal. The large rope-drum is then disconnected from the engine, the engine stopped, and two workmen push the empty boat off the wagon, put on a full one instead, and attach the wagon to the chain of the small drum. This chain was unwound during the time that the empty boat was passing over the ridge, at which time also the chain-drum was connected with the engine. As soon as the full boat is pushed on, the engine is started, and, by means of the chain, draws the full boat upwards out of the canal on to the ridge of the self-acting plane. One workman stands at the engine, the other at the brake. As soon as the boat is across, it is attached to the rope of the large drum and let down the plane by means of the brake. To permit this, the engine is stopped, and the chain drum disconnected from it; this done, the workman removes the chain from the wagon and puts on the brake, keeping it on until the full boat plunges into the water at the lower canal. In between, a workman has time to attend to the firing of the engine, and to bring the boats into position and attach them, so that little time is lost. The workman at the lower canal is also employed in the unloading &c. as affixing and detaching the boats requires little time. At Coalport on the lower canal a ton of coal costs 8s., a very low price when the fact that already the coal has come from the pit many miles distant is taken into consideration.

All the connection wheels of the brake arrangement are cast in two parts, which reduces the danger of breakage when they are being staked on their axles. The axles are of cast iron 4 in. square, the journals $3\frac{1}{2}$ in. diameter, the wheels 3 in. in the split part. The engine crank is 18 in. long. The rope which lets down the wagons is $3\frac{1}{2}$ in. diameter. The large rope drum makes $\frac{1}{4}$ of a revolution for one revolution of the engine shaft, and the small chain drum makes 7/48 or about 1/7 of a revolution . . .

XXVIII

Charles Hulbert, the Shrewsbury cotton master, draper, auctioneer and bookseller, published many books on Shropshire and the history of the county. He was an Evangelical who was well acquainted with Mary Fletcher of Madeley. His account of the Severn Gorge in one of his principal works is valuable in several respects, for his count of river barges at Coalport, for his splendid description of the busy-ness of the Gorge, and for his observation of the demolition of the Calcutts ironworks. Many of the business and professional activities he noted in Ironbridge can still be observed there today.

Source: Charles Hulbert, *The History and Description of the County of Salop*, 1837, pp. 343–48.

Coalport, equal in importance to many towns, is celebrated for its rich and extensive China Works, which have for 40 years, been established here by Messrs. John Rose and Co. The articles produced at this Manufactory are not surpassed, in taste, elegance, and durability, by any in our nation or foreign countries, giving employment to 800 hands, and enrich the vicinity.

There are no places of Public Worship here, except a Methodist Chapel. A very handsome Iron Bridge, erected in 1817, crosses the Severn—from which, in May 1836, I counted no fewer than seventy two vessels loading and unloading their various cargoes, chiefly Coal, of which 50,000 tons are carried down the river annually. A commodious Warehouse, five stories in height, has been erected by the Lord of the Manor from whence proceed and return vessels for Worcester, Gloucester, Bristol, etc.

A little above Coalport is the Inclined Plane, which, by the facility it affords in loading and unloading vessels, may be said to connect Shropshire Canal with the River Severn. To the late W. Reynolds, Esq., the whole neighbourhood, and indeed all this vast district of Coal Works, Iron Works and Canals, is deeply indepted for its great prosperity. At the summit of the inclined Plane is the Hay, the residence of John Rose, Esq., of the Porcelain Manufactory, commanding most extraordinary and delightful views—A short distance from the house stands an ancient Lime Tree—its capacious hollow trunk would hold 20 persons. Some distance below the Hay is the beautiful residence of William Anstice, Esq., Mayor of Wenlock, a gentleman of distinguished taste and geological knowledge. His collection of the

49. *'the Shropshire Canal is united with the Severn by a self-acting plane 793 ft. long
and with a vertical drop of 207 ft. or an angle of 15½ degrees....'* (C. von Oeynhausen
and H. von Dechen, 1826-7)

The Hay inclined plane, Coalport, after partial restoration, 1972

Photo: The Author

fossils of the country is matchless, enriched also with specimens from
distant Britain, and foreign districts.

From Coalport to the Ironbridge, two miles, the river passes through the
most extraordinary district in the world: the banks on each side are elevated
to the height of from 3 to 400 feet, studded with Iron Works, Brickworks,
Boat Building Establishments, Retail Stores, Inns, and Houses, perhaps 150
vessels on the river, actively employed or waiting for cargoes; while hundreds
and hundreds of busy mortals are assiduously engaged, melting with the heat,
of the roaring furnace; and though enveloped in thickest smoke and incessant
dust are cheerful and happy. Madeley Wood is also a very populous portion
of the parish in which is a spacious Methodist Chapel and the extensive
Iron Works of the Madeley Wood Company.

100

Ironbridge. Here we may say is the merchantile part of the town of Madeley, and here is the focus of professional and commercial pursuits. The Weekly Market, the Post Office, the Printing Office, principal inns, Drapery, Grocery and Ironmongery, Watch Making, Cabinet Making, Timber and Boat Building establishments; the Subscription Library, Subscription Dispensary, Branch Bank Subscription Baths, Gentlemen of the Legal and Medical Professions, Ladies' Boarding School, etc., etc. Navigation being also, as previously intimated, carried on to a very considerable extent, gives to Ironbridge the character and appearance of an inland port.

Passing from Ironbridge to Coalbrookdale, on the right are three excellent inns, and also Houses and Stores; on the left, overlooking the river, is Benthall Edge, with the Lime and Stone Quarries, its inclined plane, and thousands of flourishing fir trees. The Dale, as it is generally called, is, and for ages may be eminent, as containing the most extensive ironworks in the whole world—the present Coalbrookdale Company employ more than two thousand hands here and at Horsehay.

(*In Jackfield*) is the ruinated mansion of the Tuckies within little more than half a century the residence of that admirable Chemist and enterprising nobleman Lord Dundonald, who died so recently as 1831. At the Calcutts on the banks of the Severn, his Lordship constructed ovens, stoves, &c. for the extraction of tar from coals . . . On the site of the Earl's operation was erected the great iron foundry, where so many cannon were cast by Mr. Brodies during the late war—two of which now on the premises (August 1836) are to be devoted to the furnace as old metal. Mr. Hazeldine occupied a foundry here for 14 years, but such was the unpropitiousness of the period, even his master talents could not ensure success—he consequently lost some thousands in the adventure. At the period of my visit, the proprietor, Mr. Foster, 'the great iron master' had men engaged in removing all the erections formerly in occupation as a foundry. Near to Calcutts are the extensive works of Mr. William Davies, where at least 900,000 flooring bricks and tiles besides malting tiles, firebricks etc. are annually manufactured. The articles here produced at the adjacent works, and in the parish of Madeley, are not surpassed by any in the kingdom; heavy as the bricks etc. are, they find ready markets along the whole course of the River Severn, up the Avon and even in foreign countries . . . A short way down the river and near its verge is the New Pottery of brown and yellow stone ware, belonging to Mr. John Myatt—he kindly took me round his works and explained the whole process of manufacture. The various produce of his art and skill appeared of excellent quality. In this vicinity are also various manufactories of rope, oil, etc.

XXIX

Primitive Methodism was established in the Shropshire coalfield by missionaries from the Potteries during a great revival in 1821-22. A chapel was erected at Wrockwardine Wood which became the centre of a powerful and influential circuit, from which other parts of Shropshire and more distant areas were missioned. Revivals were a feature of the religious life of the coalfield amongst all sorts of Methodists. They seem to have fulfilled a deep seated emotional need among people who were accustomed to a dangerous and violent working environment. The description which follows is of one of the incidents in the sustained revival of the late 1830s and early 40s, from the journal of John Moore, Primitive Methodist minister at Wrockwardine Wood from 1838-41. Moore had long wished to be stationed at Wrockwardine Wood, and during his ministry the Primitive Methodists extended their activities into the southern half of the coalfield around Dawley and Madeley, and established societies in the rural area to the north of Wellington.

Source: *Primitive Methodist Magazine,* 1841, pp. 154-55.

Sunday August 4 (1839).
Held our Wrockwardine Wood (circuit) Camp meeting. This was held upon a large cinder hill, near to Donnington Wood blast furnaces. First, we put all the Sunday scholars in order, processioned about twenty minutes, and then we proceeded to the Camp ground. While engaged in prayer at the opening of the meeting, the people rose unitedly into the exercise of mighty faith; the feeling was heavenly, and at times almost overpowering. Nor did that blessed and powerful influence leave the meeting the whole of the day. The hearts of both the preachers and people were fixed upon God; and divine and eternal things seemed fully to captivate every soul. All the preachings, exhortations, singing, and praying, were attended with such a degree of Divine Unction, that it was clearly discovered (and felt) that the arm of the Lord was revealed. The congregation was much larger in the morning than ordinary. And in the afternoon, this populous country appeared all on the move. The people came crowding in from every quarter, till the congregation soon consisted of about four thousand persons.
We divided into four companies for prayer every time we went out. we had an abundance of prayer, faith was kept alive, the powers of hell were driven, the people were deeply serious, and the Holy Ghost descended on the whole.

50. *'Here, we may say is the merchantile part of the town of Madeley, and here is the focus of professional and commercial pursuits. . . .'* (Charles Hulbert, 1836)

The Square, Ironbridge, 1976

Photo: The Author

51. *'. . . Drapery, Grocery establishments. . . .'* (Charles Hulbert, 1836)

Part of Letterhead of Edward Edwards, Linen & Woollen Draper of Ironbridge, 1841

Ironbridge Gorge Museum Trust

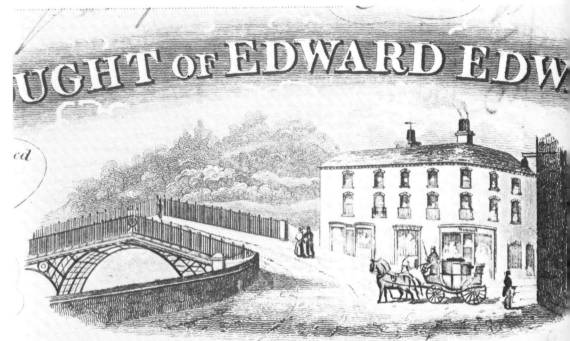

The people were at this, as well as at all our other Camp meetings, constantly exhorted to exercise living faith in the Great Atonement, and keep a present salvation in view; and this I believe was duly attended to. We broke up about five o'clock p.m., and at six o'clock commenced the lovefeast in our Wrockwardine Wood chapel. It was soon crowded to excess, both in the gallery and in the bottom. And the Lord, in answer to united prayer, so filled the chapel with his glorious presence, that the congregation was shaken throughout. The speaking was powerful, and it went on well until sinners were brought into such deep distress of soul on account of their lost state, that we were obliged to turn in into a prayer meeting. The most distressing cries for mercy were very soon heard from every part of the chapel, in the gallery and below; so that there was full employment for all who knew the Lord.

As speedily as possible four penitent forms were placed, and the mourners and broken-hearted were invited to come forward to be prayed for. Many came forward voluntarily, and fell down before the Lord; others were in such deep distress as to become almost helpless, and these were brought forward. Care was particularly taken that persons of piety and experience, and who understood something of the mystery of faith, were engaged to pray with the penitents, and only one at a time were allowed to speak to each mourner, and all in the chapel were exhorted to be engaged heavily with God, and in and through all to fully believe in Christ Jesus for a present salvation. The praying was truly mighty; and, though at all times, hell would try to prevail, we were enabled to push the battle to the gate. The Holy Ghost so filled all, that amidst cries for mercy, bursts of halleluias, mighty praying, and praising God, it was all harmonious and divinely solemn. At my two penitent forms, eighteen or twenty previous souls obtained a solid sense of sins forgiven, and were delivered from sin and satan's power; and near that number found the like blessing at the other forms, and others went away in distress. This has been a great day: language fails to express what I felt on this occasion. Halleluia! halleluia for ever! the Lord God Omnipotent reigneth. All glory to the Lamb of God.

XXX

John Randall (1810–1910) was a native of Broseley who became one of the most celebrated china painters of his day, specialising in the painting of birds. He was employed at the china works at Coalport, where he lived for a period, but by 1871 he had moved to Madeley where he kept the Post Office, and ran a printing and bookselling business. He published numerous works on local history and geology, based on his own reading, research and reminiscences. His first major venture as an author seems to have been a long series of articles on 'The Severn Valley' in the Shrewsbury Chronicle *in 1859, which formed the basis of his first book, of the same title, which appeared in 1862, and of many of his later works. The extracts which follow include numerous details which do not appear in his books.*

Source: Articles on The Severn Valley, by John Randall in *Shrewsbury Chronicle,* April–June 1859.

(The River Severn) . . . Shrewsbury, Coalbrookdale, Coalport, Bridgnorth, Bewdley Stourport, Worcester and Gloucester are centres from which its traffic flows, iron crude and malleable, brick and tile, earthenware and pipes, are sent; the former in large quantities from wharfs at Coalbrookdale and from others between Ironbridge and Coalport. From the latter the amount of tonnage for the last years, including imports and exports was as follows:—

1827	..	79,323
1837	..	66,589
1847	..	67,747
1857	..	48,680

The whole annual amount of the Shropshire trade is from 40,000 to 50,000 tons, chiefly of the mineral produce of the district. That between Stourport and Gloucester is supposed to be 250,000 or 300,000 more. The Shropshire trade is carried on by means of vessels from 40 to 78 tons burthen, drawing from three to four feet which go down with the stream, and are drawn back by horses. In consequence of the rapidity of the current over the fords, not more than 20, 30, or to tons are usually carried up the river. About 20 voyages in the year are usually made by regular traders, but vessels carrying iron make more. The time occupied for full cargoes to get down to Gloucester is 24 hours . . . Traffic upon the Severn is said to cost less than upon any other in the kingdom . . . Till within a few years back no attempts at improvement similar to those made in other rivers . . . had been made, otherwise a larger traffic may probably at this moment have been carried

105

52. 'Coalport . . . is the creation of energies that found their development as symbols of industrial enterprise came to be higher prized than those of war . . . a landscape not unpleasing . . . when not obscured by smoke. . . .' (John Randall, 1859)

Coalport from the top of the Hay inclined plane, 1973

Photo: The Author

53. '. . . here we are at the pit's mouth . . . the chains busy over the pulleys tink-a-tink-tink, clat-clat-clattering over the rollers, increasing the width of its coils and the rate of its speed. . . .' (John Randall, 1859)

A winding engine belonging to the Coalbrookdale Company in the Lightmoor area, c. 1880

Ironbridge Gorge Museum Trust

on . . . As a class, barge-owners are opposed to innovations, and act too much upon superannuated maxims that bolt and bar out improvements. The oldest men on the river remember how, 'when George the Third was king', they shouted themselves hoarse and tossed their caps in honour of victory over attempts to improve the channel . . . As it is, there are often three, four and five months in the year, when barges cannot navigate the river with a freight equal to defray the expenses of working them; indeed instances have occurred in which only two months of the twelve the river could be advantageously worked. Within the past nine months vessels capable of carrying 50 or 60 tons got fast in the shoals with 15 . . . The Severn carriers of Shropshire . . . Have contributed to the decline of their traffic by malpractices that are notorious. There are noble exceptions; some honest-hearted fellows among the owners and the men. The true waterman is primitive in his habits, a waiter upon Providence, who will stand for months looking into the stream patiently waiting for a 'fresh' to carry him down. You may tell him by his appearance. He has a broad back, legs which a flunky may be jealous of—swelled like skittle pins at the calves, he is a hard drinker, a heavy swearer, given to gasconade and good living . . . He is clever in playing tricks with his freight. He often gets game, and frequently dines off fowl that, somehow or other find their way on board as he lies at anchor for the night. To hear him talk, the difficulties of a voyage to the East Indies is nothing to those of captaining a barge to the mouth of the Avon or the Wye . . .

. . . Rock-house, the residence of William Frederick Rose, Esq., with its aviaries, greenhouses, ornamental grounds and natural amphitheatre of rocks, stands upon the margin (of the river) . . . The elegant structure now uniting both banks of the river a little above, although of iron, is called the Wooden-bridge, from the fact that its crachy predecessor was built of that material; also to distinguish it from one two miles higher up, the first of its kind, and which gave its name to the town its erection called into existence. A large warehouse abutting upon the river above the bridge, suspended trams from the wharf, barges receiving cargoes or, having loaded, waiting for sufficient water to carry them over the fords; the clang of iron as it is transferred from boats upon the canal to vessels on the river, and huge black stacks of mineral fuel upon the banks, moreover, suggest the name of the place at which we have arrived . . . Coalport has no venerable ruins or historical associations to tempt us; it has neither been the battle ground of hostile races nor contending dynasties,—but is the creation of energies that found their development as symbols of industrial enterprise came to be higher prized than those of war. Within the memory of the oldest inhabitant it was in a state of nature-fieldless, roadless, with one solitary habitation where cultured slopes, cottages, gardens, wharfs and workshops meet the eye . . . Vessels on the river, cottages clustering on the hill sides, the old Italian-looking villa at the Tuckies, round upland knolls and rocky cliffs, with the Wrekin half-hidden in the distance, present a landscape not unpleasing—we ought, perhaps, to say when not obscured by smoke . . . the grim-looking factory, its bottle-shaped hovels, its white china heaps, its black smoke columns, . . . Above the works a little ferry plying from side to side with toil-freed artizans, hastening to meals, or, answering the brazen summons of the bell to renew their labour . . .

. . . one of the Madeley Wood Company's pits . . . You may go down in the 'doubles' or in the 'skip'. In the former you are seated upon a small round chain; in the latter case, you stand upright in a basket. The men prefer the former, and go down swing and singing in a bunch—ten or twenty men and boys at a time . . . here we are at the pit's mouth . . . men, women and boys all at work, and the chains busy over the pulleys tink-a-tink-tink, clat-clat-clattering over the rollers, increasing the width of its coils and the rate of its speed, as the load at the end nears the surface. You have donn'd a flannel frock, and are altogether transmogrified by a short round skull cap. A platform on wheels is run over the mouth of the shaft to allow you to get in. By special favour the under-ground bailiff accompanies you, and his presence secures respect. A group of pit girls and boys pass a sly joke at your expense, and a hope is expressed that you will pay your foot-ale. At a motion of the hand by your guide you are snatched up in an instant, the platform slides from under, and suddenly you find yourself with nothing but thin air for a distance twice or thrice the height of St. Paul's below you . . . rattle, rattle, rattle,—puff, bang, and clatter, clatter, clatter, reminds you that you are at the mercy of machinery. You are nervous, and regret your temerity; feeling like a falling body in vacuum. The orifice of the shaft fast diminishes to a day-star; or, with the fast revolving pulley at the top, looks like a burnt-out pyrotechnic wheel on a dark night. You feel to be standing on a column of thin vapour, that now assails your nostrils with mingled smells, as down, down goes the skip on which you stand, and you follow by virtue of your own weight. Drops of water patter on your head, coal dust fills your eyes; the ascending load shoots upwards, and soon a glimmering light from the bottom points out the limit of your descent. A sense of motion in the extreme darkness of the lower portion of the pit is lost, but ascending whiffs and earthy smells that assail the nostrils remind you of the fact, while a bump upon touching the bottom-which makes it appear as though the earth suddenly lifted itself up—convinces you. Well, here you are, in less than time that it has taken us to describe the descent, at the entrance of the works, standing on another wooden platform, or false bottom to the shaft, which covers the 'sump' into which trickle the waste waters that leak from the mine. A load of coals is hung on to the chain, you have left, and you commit your self once more to the basket, to which are fitted four narrow wheels that run on rails. A sleek pit pony is hook to, the 'jockey' seated in front, gives a crack of his whip, a 'Gee-up Fanny', and you are off at a trot. You have a candle, stuck into a bit of moist clay—a very convenient candlestick, too, for a mine, seeing that you can fasten it to the sides or anywhere you like. With this,

54. '... *the grim-looking factory, its bottle-shaped hovels, its white china heaps, its black smoke columns*. . . .' (John Randall, 1859)

The Coalport china works, *c.* **1900**

Ironbridge Gorge Museum Trust

55. *A 'toil-freed artisan'* (John Randall, 1859)

John Randall (1810-1910) in old age

Ironbridge Gorge Museum Trust

vour eyes having become accustomed to the gloom, you can now explore the mine. You pass the stables, which in a pit have a curious indescribable smell. You observe the roof bulging in and bending down the cross-timbers that rest on stout upright 'trees' for support. Here and there, it may be, are hollows where, having been disturbed by older works in strata a storey higher up, it has fallen in, forming dark caverns, in which explosive gas accumulates. Touch it with a candle, and it will flash like gun-cotton, in blue flames along the roof. A door, kept by a boy who sits all day pent up in darkness to perform this monotonous duty, opens to admit us. We come in sight of boys called 'foals' in gear called 'mobbeys', drawing coals or 'spoil' to the waggons. These appear like imps; while men, naked to the waist, toiling in deep twilight and black coal-dust, wielding picks and maundrels, look full-grown demons. The atmosphere is oppressive, and you perspire freely as you find yourself in the inner recesses of the mine. The 'holders', or hewers, are squatting on their haunches, lying on their sides, stooping and bending two double to get out the underclay or 'pricking' from beneath the beds of coals. It is these uncouth positions that make them look as though they had sat as long astride a barrel as Simon Stylites is said to have done upon a pillar to a less useful end. The getters are those who bring down the minerals when undermined. Blasting is resorted to where naked lights burn clear, and the works free from fire-damp, at which time the booming echoes along the galleries and subterranean recesses of the mine with a supernatural sound . . .

XXXI

The industrial village of Coalbrookdale was a most unusual settlement.
In the 18th century a whole succession of important innovations in iron-
making were made there, and a high tradition of craftsmanship was
preserved in the 19th century, exemplified by the fine art castings produced
in the foundry. A host of ancient traditions was preserved there, and some
were recalled in a talk given by Charles Peskin, then a very old man, to the
Caradoc and Severn Valley Field Club in April 1941.

Source: *Transactions of the Caradoc and Severn Valley Field Club,* Vol. XI,
1941; 'Memories of Old Coalbrookdale', by Charles F. Peskin (extracts
from paper read 25 April 1941).

Looking back nearly 70 years, I notice how games, pastimes and diversions
have changed. When I was a schoolboy in the early 'seventies we used to
play at tipcat, dogger, murky, bandy, prison bars, spiking the spinning
top—games one rarely if ever sees now. Even the marbles games are different.
We had iron taws, skimmers and tinkers, which when shied at the 'puds'
or 'cogs' would sometimes knock the whole lot down. And we would erect
catsgallows for leaping, with hazel sticks. Girls' games—skipping, tut-ball,
and five stones—are perhaps still played, except the last-named.

*   *   *   *   *   *   *

. . . There were other disgraceful exploits we engaged in sometimes, such as
'Burning the Mawkin'. At the instigation of older ones, who no doubt
assisted us, we would make an effigy of straw and old clothes, and then
form a procession, and with tin whistles, clappers and tin cans for music
we would carry the 'mawkin' to the door of a wife-beater and fire it. We
were told the man had been doing some 'threshing' and had some short
straw for sale.

It was not unusual in the early seventies for dilatory and presumably idle
workmen—fellows who persistently lost morning 'quarters'—to be fetched
forcibly from home, put in a wheel-barrow, and, in the middle of a procession accompanied with tin cans, gongs, whistles, rattles and anything noisy,
conveyed triumphantly to the foundry and upset there. This was called
'ringing them in.'

*   *   *   *   *   *   *

Most housewives did their own laundry-work and baking, and some brewed
their own beer. The barm for baking could be obtained on certain days at

111

any of the inns, and small beer could be had for 3d. a bucketful, which made a good dinner beverage. The washing had to be taken to the mangle-room, which was a noted gossiping place. Water for domestic use had to be carried to most of the houses in the Upper Dale, from the Bathwell pump or from the pump which used to be in the foundry. This was the only supply of clean water, except for a few lucky ones who had wells. Many women carried their own water from the pumps, and it was not unusual to see a woman carrying a pail of water on her head, supported by a round cloth pad. Coal was fetched from the coal-pen in half-hundredweights or hundredweights, which cost 4d. per hundredweight for coal and 2d. per hundredweight for slack (not dirt, but small cobbles or nuts). The Coalbrookdale Company mined their own pits at Dawley and Lightmoor, whence the coal was brought down the 'jenny rails' in flat carriages, stacked up and held in position by huge hoops made in a rectangular shape to suit the wagons. The drivers of the horses and waggons had large wooden pegs to scotch the wheels when coming too fast.

When I began work sixty-six years ago, there was an old man named John Aston living in the Strawbarn, who had been married four times. He was generally known as Drummer Aston and his last wife, who, he declared, was the best of the four, he 'bought' at Wenlock fair for 1s. 6d. and brought her to Coalbrookdale with a halter-rope round her neck; this was supposed to clinch the bargain.

XXXII

In the mid–19th century the Shropshire iron industry had lost the pre-eminence it had enjoyed in earlier years, but it remained a sizeable industry. This newspaper account of the visit of the Iron and Steel Institute is important for the detailed description of the ultra-modern enterprises of the Lilleshall Company, for the impression it gives of Henry Bessemer leading the party at great speed around the Coalbrookdale ironworks, for quotations from ironworks records which are now lost, and for the information about the first steam railway locomotive built at Coalbrookdale by Richard Trevithick about 1802. The final comment by Mr. Anstice was a fitting epitaph on the Shropshire iron trade, which entered a period of precipitate decline not long afterwards.

Source: *Eddowes Salopian Journal,* 6 September 1871.

The Iron and Steel Institute Visit to Shropshire on Friday.

Shropshire, from its position outside the great central mining and manufacturing district of the Midland Counties, is apt to escape the attention of scientific men, and those interested in observing the progress made in those great industries. Nevertheless, it has a past history full of interest, many of its early ironmasters were pioneers of improvements, to whom later ones are indebted all over the country, and it has at the same time evidence to show that it is doing its best to keep pace with other parts of the country. The more important of the Shropshire works are those of Lilleshall and Coalbrookdale, and to visit these the members of the Institute proceeded by special train along the Great Western Railway line to Hollinswood, where a junction is formed with the Lilleshall Company's mineral railway, by which they were conveyed, with one of the Company's engines, direct to the Priorslee furnaces, and through the Priorslee colliery district to the Lodge or Donnington Wood field, thence to the mills, forges and engine shops . . .

In the Priorslee district there are ten pairs of pits; in the Donnington Wood district twenty one pairs; and in the Hadley field nine pairs. The magnitude of the company's operations may be better understood by stating that the coal and slack raised amount to 420,000 tons per annum; the ironstone raised and purchased to 120,000 tons, and the debris in connection with the latter to 700,000.

56. *'At the Lodge . . . (the) . . . blast furnaces or huge cones constructed for the purpose of melting down the ores. . . .'* (Eddowes Salopian Journal, 1871)

The Lilleshall Company's Lodge Furnaces in Shropshire

From Samuel Griffiths' 'Guide to the Iron Trade of Great Britain', 1873

57. *'. . . we enter the forges and engine sheds, to see, by cunning manipulation, the metal converted into objects of use and beauty. . . .'* (Eddowes Salopian Journal, 1871)

The Lilleshall Company's Great Foundry and Engine Factory (the New Yard works at St. George's, Oakengates)

From Samuel Griffiths' 'Guide to the Iron Trade of Great Britain', 1873

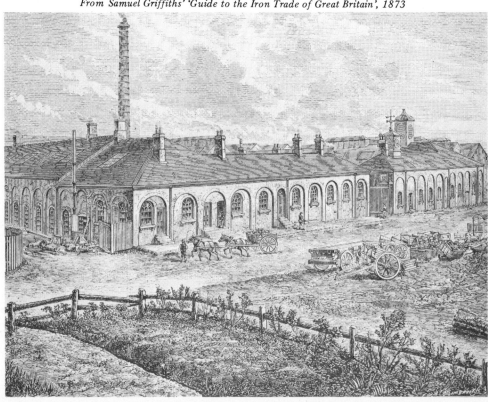

The machinery everywhere employed is of the most approved construction, and railways are seen running in all directions through the field, connecting the collieries with the furnaces, these with the engine sheds, uniting each with the other, and all with the Great Western Railway on the south side, with the London and North Western Railway on the north, and with the Shropshire Union Canal on the north west.

At the Lodge . . . the . . . blast furnaces or huge cones constructed for the purpose of melting down the ores are altogether nine in number, eight of which are in blast, and the average make is 1,400 tons per week. An additional twenty feet of brickwork has been added to the necks of these great crucibles here raising them to seventy feet in height, effecting considerable economy in heat and fuel. They are kept in operation by a pair of blowing giants built upon the model of those so much admired in the Exhibition of 1862. The steam cylinders are 40 in. and the blowing cylinders 86 in. in diameter. The engines have an 8½ ft. stroke, and the steam pressure is 35 lbs., cut off at one fourth of the stroke, and working high pressure. There are six boilers, two tubes to each. A portion of the coke is prepared in ovens, of which there are fifty, in which small coal or slack is utilised. It is first washed, and the coke, upon being withdrawn, is also watered by perforated pipes. Three calcining kilns, 40 ft. in height and 26 ft. in diameter cased with iron plates, are used to prepare the ore, which is raised to the top by an inclined plane, and by means of a small engine . . .

. . . and now having followed the materials from the gloom of ages to the light of day, from the pits to the smelting furnaces, we enter the forges and engine sheds, to see, by cunning manipulation, the metal converted into objects of use and beauty. Here are rolling mills where the iron is pressed into the shapes required by rapidly revolving cylinders of immense power. White hot and elastic, it is caught with tongs and passed and re-passed till it comes out a broad flat plate fit for an ironclad, or a long square bar, to be used or cut up for other purposes. In the machine shop are sixty five planing, turning, boring, shaping, slotting, drilling and slot rolling machines. There are also large fitting and erecting shops, used for the making of locomotives and engines of all kinds. Here we found large pumping engines with 72 in. cylinders for the Birmingham Water Works Company. These engines will have a stroke of 11 ft. We also observed a pair of winding engines for the Forest of Dean. The Company are also just completing Nettlefold and Chamberlain's rolling mill and Siemens regenerating gas furnaces, which will be the first of the kind erected here and will prove a great novelty in the district.

There were also some of the machinery and plant connected with the blast furnaces the company have been preparing for Russia. Before leaving St. George's, the party partook of some bitter beer and biscuits which Mr. Horton had thoughtfully provided, and a kindness, we need scarcely repeat, which was heartily appreciated.

From the engine sheds the party returned to Hollinswood, and thence by the Great Western line, the Naird, and Madeley Court, to the Albert Edward bridge erected by the Coalbrookdale Company over the Severn where the party alighted to admire the scenery, as well as the sight of the first bridge of iron erected in the world, which is seen at a little distance, and several went down to have a nearer view. A visit was then paid to the works, where considerable admiration was expressed with regard to the sharpness, cleanness and crispness of the castings. Having gone through a portion of the works, Mr. Norris and Mr. Bessemer leading the way, the party began to think about luncheon, which now awaited them in the large room of the Institute. Some time was profitably spent, however, in the Reading room where a number of objects of interest were exhibited. Among the early productions shown to the visitors of these celebrated works, were some iron pots, used for domestic purposes, one of which had the date 1717, with the initials H.E. It appears from the Blast Furnace Memorandum Book of Abraham Darby that the make of iron at the Coalbrookdale foundry, in 1713, varied from 5 to 10 tons per week. The principal items cast were pots, kettles and other 'hollow ware', direct from the smelting furnace; the rest of the metal was run into pigs. In the course of time we find that other castings were turned out, a few grates, smoothing irons, door frames, etc. Sugar pans afterwards became a great article of commerce and then steam engines . . . A number of photographs were exhibited by Mr. William Reynolds Anstice of the Madeley Wood Company, of inventions and contrivances by a former proprietor of those works, William Reynolds, who succeeded his father, Richard Reynolds, in the Ketley Works. Among them was a boiler, firebox, and other parts of the machinery which belonged to a locomotive invented by William Reynolds, and which is believed to have been the first, but a fatal accident happening upon starting the machinery, the jury threatened a heavy fine upon Mr. Reynolds for every day it was used, and the consequence was that it was abandoned. This was before the machine invented by Trevithick travelled for a short time at a slow rate with heavy loads at Merthyr; and, it is believed, even before Symington exhibited his model of the steam carriage in Edinburgh. Another invention of Mr. Reynolds was shown by a photograph of the well known inclined plant at Coalport, devised by him for the purpose of overcoming the irregularities of the surface when canal navigation was of much more importance to the iron districts of Shropshire than at present, and by means of which boats laden with coal or iron were let down from one canal to another 207 ft. below, the lower one being close upon the banks of the Severn. Mr. Telford, the eminent engineer, described some years ago this contrivance very fully; other engineers have also spoken highly of this invention, which was figured upon the copper tokens of the time.

Some photographs and drawings were also exhibited of some primitive looking engines with wooden beams now in use and which have been in use in the Madeley Wood field for many years. They are called Adams

58. '. . . Mr. Norris and Mr. Bessemer leading the way, the party began to think about luncheon which now awaited them in the large room of the Institute. . . .' (Eddowes Salopian Journal, 1871)

The Institute, Coalbrookdale

Photo: Ironbridge Gorge Museum

59. '. . . Another invention of Mr. Reynolds was . . . the well known inclined plane at Coalport. . . .' (Eddowes Salopian Journal, 1871)

The Hay Inclined Plane, Coalport, 1976, following restoration of the rails and the bottom basin

Photo: The Author

engines, from the fact that they were constructed by a man named Adam Heslop. They differ from the ordinary condensing engine of Boulton and Watt in having a cylinder at each end—one a steam cylinder and the other a condensing one—into which the steam having done its duty in one cylinder is conveyed.

There were a number of specimens of firebricks and other productions of the different clays obtained from the Coalbrookdale Company's field; also terra cotta vases and other ornaments. The Messrs. Maw and Hargreaves, Craven Dunnill and Co. exhibited some very superior tesselated and encaustic tiles. The former firm had some very fine specimens—majolica and various ornaments in coloured glazes. Messrs. John Rose and Co. of Coalport, contributed a magnificent collection of their more recent productions, which were very much admired. At luncheon, which was a really sumptuous one, W. O. Foster, Esq., presided, supported on his right by Mr. Bessemer . . .

. . . The toasts having been duly honoured, Mr. Bessemer in responding, said the iron trade of the world had learnt a great deal from Shropshire, and he had experienced a great deal of pleasure in inspecting those old works where had been inaugurated and successfully carried out some of the most important and useful improvements of which the iron trade could boast . . .

. . . Mr. Anstice (of Madeley Wood) in proposing 'the Iron Trades of Great Britain', said that while the ironmasters of Shropshire could not but feel deeply gratified at the compliments paid them by Mr. Bessemer—a name, he said of world wide celebrity, it became them to recollect that although Shropshire was among the oldest, it was no longer among the largest seats of that great national industry, which, commencing in Sussex, thence spreading to Staffordshire and Shropshire, had now extended throughout the length and breadth of the land, other districts had passed them in the race, and Shropshire, he feared, was somewhat in the position of a man who, while conscious that his own best days were past, regarded with pride the race of giant sons which had grown up around him.

XXXIII

The 20th century has been a period of economic decline in the Severn Gorge. The last ironworks in the immediate vicinity of the Gorge, that at Blists Hill, ceased operation in 1912. One by one the brick and tile works in the area have stopped working, and numerous other industries have disappeared. It is largely due to this decline that so many outstandingly important monuments of the Industrial Revolution have survived in the district, although until quite recently they were sadly neglected. In an article in 1955, in which the term 'Industrial Archaeology' was used in print for the first time, Michael Rix called for a greater appreciation of the bridges, factories and other monuments of the 18th and 19th centuries. He picked out the Severn Gorge as an area where there were great opportunities for the preservation of industrial monuments, defining the task which, in 1968, the Ironbridge Gorge Museum Trust was created to fulfil.

Source: Michael Rix, 'Industrial Archaeology', in *The Amateur Historian,* Vol. II, 1955, pp. 225-29.

Great Britain as the birthplace of the Industrial Revolution is full of monuments left by this remarkable series of events. Any other country would have set up machinery for the scheduling and preservation of these memorials that symbolise the movement which is changing the face of the globe, but we are so oblivious of our national heritage that apart from a few museum pieces, the majority of these landmarks are neglected or unwittingly destroyed . . .

. . . the cradle of this movement which is still thickly sown with monuments is the small valley, Coalbrookdale, on the edge of the Severn Gorge in Eastern Shropshire. Here in Queen Anne's reign a Quaker—Abraham Darby— first smelted iron with coke, and part of the furnace that he bought, dated 1657, can still be seen. The pioneer work in Coalbrookdale in the 18th century makes impressive reading. The first cast iron holloware, the first iron railway, the first hot blast furnace, the first iron bridge (which gives its name to nearby Ironbridge), the first commercial locomotive head the list, which includes the manufacture of cylinders for James Watt's improved steam engine and the elimination of locks from canals by the use of inclined planes. The iron bridge erected in 1779 which still spans the Severn although it is now closed to traffic. The furnace in which the mammoth ribs were cast can still be seen and is to be preserved . . .

60. *'The iron bridge erected in 1779 . . . still spans
the Severn. . . .'* (Michael Rix, 1955)
The Iron Bridge, 1975
Photo: D. Fry

. . . there are still many monuments to be scheduled, many books to be
written and much field work to be done before industrial archaeology
can begin to take its rightful place among the studies of these islands.

61. *'. . . many monuments to be scheduled . . . much field work to be done. . . .'* (Micha
Rix, 195

The North Engine House, and the excavated remains of the blast furnaces, at the Blists Hill op
air museum, 19
Photo: D. F

120

FURTHER READING

The most complete account of the social and economic history of the Shropshire coalfield is Barrie Trinder, *The Industrial Revolution in Shropshire* (Phillimore, 1973), which is fully referenced, and contains an extensive bibliography. The same author's *The Darby's of Coalbrookdale* (Phillimore, 1974) is a short, popular account of one of the principal families of ironmasters. Arthur Raistrick's *Dynasty of Ironfounders* (1953) is by now a classic of industrial history, but omits many sources which have come to light in the last two decades. Neil Cossons and Barrie Trinder, *The Iron Bridge* (forthcoming) will provide a definitive account of the building of the bridge and its impact both nationally and locally.

The Ironbridge Gorge Museum publishes a range of site guides, many of them to places which were also much visited in the 18th century, including the Coalbrookdale ironworks, the Hay inclined plane, the Iron Bridge, the Tar Tunnel and the Coalport chinaworks. The Museum also publishes *A Description of Coalbrookdale in 1801,* a detailed account by an anonymous local resident, edited by Barrie Trinder. The various works of the 19th-century Madeley writer, John Randall, particularly *The Severn Valley* (1862 and 1882), *The History of Madeley* (1880, reprinted with a new introduction by Barrie Trinder, 1975), and the chapters on industry in the *Victoria History of Shropshire,* Vol I (1908), still contain much of value, but are far from reliable.

Trevor Rowley, *The Shropshire Landscape* (1972) provides a broad historical introduction to the county as a whole, while Neil Cossons, *The B.P. Book of Industrial Archaeology* (1975) is a copious work of reference on industrial processes and a useful guide to surviving monuments throughout Great Britain. For early mining in Shropshire, see J. U. Nef, *The Rise of the British Coal Industry* (1932) and for later mining, Ivor J. Brown, *The Mines of Shropshire* (1976). For primitive railways the standard work is M. J. T. Lewis, *Early Wooden Railways* (1970), and for standard gauge lines, Rex Christiansen, *A Regional History of the Railways of Great Britain,* Vol. 7, *The West Midlands* (1973); for canals, Charles Hadfield, *The Canals of the West Midlands* (1966); for ironmaking technology, W. K. V. Gale, *Iron and Steel* (1968); for the porcelain industry, G. A. Godden, *Caughley and Worcester Porcelains* (1969) and *Coalport and Coalbrookdale Porcelains* (1970); and for the chemical industry, A. and N. Clow, *The Chemical Revolution* (1952). F. D. Klingender, *Art and the Industrial Revolution* (1947) has useful material on the reaction of artists to the industries of the Coalbrookdale area, but does not refer to the important works which have come to light in recent years.

INDEX